I0843270

I would like to thank my wife, children, family, and friends for their unwavering support throughout my life. I am very lucky to have you.

Table of Contents

Part 1: The Basic Laws of Education

For hundreds of years the guiding principles and practices behind education have remained largely the same. We attend a school, learn from a teacher, study books, and specialize our knowledge. The standard education model has been our one-size-fits-all solution for a very long time. I believe the time has come to acknowledge that a LOT has changed the past 100 years regarding technology, understanding of human patterns, and automation. The rate of change has been steep, the knowledge attained is extensive, and the desire by governments and society to evolve has been slow.

In many countries around the world, the inaction toward development of education is largely due to budgetary constraints. In others, it is due the amount of profit being generated by the private aspects of the education system and a tangled web of misguided budgetary policy. Regardless of what type of educational impasse your country is facing, the biggest obstacle to improvement is not corporate greed or GDP line-item funding, it is efficiency. If we evolve the entire education system at once, with every improvement currently possible, the results could be astounding.

Thanks to the automation of data processing and the rise of artificial intelligence, we know what truly drives human interest and knowledge. We must take the lessons the data provides and apply them in efficient and focused processes that benefit all of society.

> *Upon the establishment of universal*
> *education practices, we can focus*
> *the entirety of our efforts on the*
> *effective communication, and*
> *efficient propagation of proven*
> *information.*

Thanks to our incredible advances in technology, we can communicate mountains of data in an instant. Each day terabits of information are generated, communicated, and later archived. With so much data at our fingertips, why haven't we been able to educate society more effectively?

Unfortunately, most of the data on the internet is either meaningless, superfluous, biased, incomplete, or just downright inaccurate. If you are over the age of 30 at time of publication, we can also safely assume that a large majority of what you learned in school has now been proven wrong by data and historical discoveries. In fact, the only thing that has remained the same over the last 30 years is basic mathematics, sort of.

The world as we knew it is no longer. Cling to our old ways we may, but the train of progress is moving on. The only solace provided from this forced lunge is derived from the knowledge that you are not alone. We all are experiencing confusion, apprehension, and the accelerating changes around us. We have drifted apart as a species and are afflicted with a temporary amnesia regarding a few of the fundamental parameters which allowed society to bloom in the first place.

- **Together we are strong.**
- **Together we can build a system that is free and fair for all.**
- **Together we can build an education system that gives back far more to society than we are required to invest.**
- **An educated society is a happier one.**

The origins of humanity, our planet, and the very nature of reality turned out to be more wonderous and fantastic than we ever imagined. Our various cultures have developed elaborate belief systems, ideologies, and local cultures that for centuries have driven a wedge into cooperative efforts. We must rise above religious and political dogma for the sake of our children. We must communicate and find common ground upon which to build the civilization of tomorrow. I am in no way forcing the issue of Globalism or speaking on its behalf, nor do I speak against its spread. I wish to preserve the cultures and practices of the world's various people so long as it does not cause societal harm. In the matter of education though, I believe a universal common ground can be identified and standardized. I humbly offer these 12 basic ideas upon which a foundation could be built.

1. The bestowal of knowledge should not be taxed, nor profited upon.
2. The flow of information and ideas should not be restricted to protect the interest of any entity.
3. The collective knowledge of humanity belongs to all of humanity.
4. We should constantly seek to improve our knowledge, quality of life, and our societal happiness.

5. At this stage in our technological evolution, education <u>IS</u> an inherent right. An individual should be allowed to go as far as their abilities and motivation allow them to.
6. By incorporating technology and utilizing multiple learning formats for each subject, a much higher information saturation percentage can be achieved.
7. An updated, private-interest-free education system would save 50% or more of the current education budget in places like the United States.
8. If you include a Merit & Achievement System, which is reportable and universal, people will strive to do more.
9. Educational paths should be less restrictive and allow an individual to develop toward their strengths instead of wasting time with generic information.
10. People respond better to content they are interested in, so let them do what they want.
11. There is more than one way to test for competency.
12. Humanity needs something to strive for. Purpose is power.

I will explain these ideas in further detail as we move on. Please note that this book is just a primer for the overall movement. You can join our effort to bring this system to reality by visiting www.EducationSolved.org By the end, I hope you'll stand ready to assist in the next chapter of our growth as a global community.

www.EducationSolved.org

Part 2: Enough of the fluff

Tell me if you've heard this one before. It's a story about the bright student who slowly lost their mind while sitting in classrooms. Within the first 10 minutes of each class they had grasped the subject matter and were doomed to spend the next 45 minutes in muted frustration. This occurred 6-7 times a day, for 12-13 years or more.

> *Our current education system is nothing more than an extended torture test.*

Mental death by boredom is how the bright stars and go-getters are extinguished in our culture. In many tech companies, it has become a running joke that all an advanced degree really means is that you are an effective follower, and content with the status quo. It is a known complication that innovators and doers have a <u>VERY</u> hard time working with slow, inefficient systems.

Efficiency matters.

In most cases, it is easy to separate good ideas from bad. For example, a reasonable mind would not manufacture food products in a saw mill. The idea of a loaf of bread being produced alongside a 2x4 is absurd. Common sense tells us that both products require different equipment, procedures, and facility conditions to optimize both their product and output.

A one-size-fits all approach is rarely the best choice, no matter what type of effort you engage in. We cannot expect maximum impact from a barrel-forward methodology, when we seek to achieve the efficient education of all 12 types of intellect our species currently exhibits. The idea of training 35 students, whose abilities, interests, and skills are wildly different, within the same classroom; is madness.

The current attitude toward education is to force us into a "well-rounded" cookie cutter mold. The system encourages mediocrity and builds a nearly insurmountable wall against achievement. This flawed, shotgun approach has produced entire generations of adults who aren't well rounded at all. In fact, according to data, people are becoming more withdrawn, less imaginative, and often feel no sense of accomplishment or belonging. As we continue our compelled compartmentalization, we feel alone, helpless, and victimized by the lack of opportunity in our society. Because we cannot reconcile our perceived failure, we turn our anger outward, blaming and even harming others as consequence. Feelings of being cast-aside by society often compound as expectations rise, and negative feelings manifest into depression, anxiety, and self-induced isolation.

To put it as simply as possible: The current system breeds mental instability, is ineffective, and requires immediate change.

Looking back on k-12 education in public schools, many children were never instructed on how to balance a checkbook. We never learned about financial responsibility, how our debt-based economy truly functioned, or about our civic responsibilities. Students aren't taught about their basic legal rights, consumer awareness, or the primary laws governing our country. My classmates didn't learn how to cook, survive in the outdoors, defend themselves, or sew a button on a shirt. Most of us were never given the opportunity to work on large-scale projects outside the standardized curriculum with fellow classmates. Given all the wonders of our society, it is a travesty that so many children in this world go their entire lives never knowing the thrill of true achievement.

But we did learn a lot of facts and dates!

Trouble is, much of what we learned as <u>FACTS</u> during the last century about History, Science, Sociology, and World Government have since been revised or disproven. Some of the FACTS we were fed were assumptions at best, and possibly propaganda at worst. I would venture to say that in 17 years of primary school, I gained roughly 2-3 years of real, applicable knowledge. By any performance measure, that's not a good result.

There is a reason billionaires and visionaries don't bother with formal education anymore.

For decades now, homeschooling and other forms of alternative education have been gaining traction. Prior to our recent technological revolution, it was only the extremely wealthy children that were guaranteed a well-rounded educational experience. For the rest of us, receiving advanced education has been a grand game of social and financial frogger. Instead of experiencing systemically planned guidance, our young children are left to fend for themselves, and their future in an unforgiving landscape. Inexperienced and naïve, we blindly stumble into the gauntlet, afraid to fail in a system rife with pitfalls. We trudge forward, knowing that we must persevere, endlessly and gracefully, all whilst attempting to avoid the mountainous obstacles in our path.

It is time that we acknowledge and address the fact that the current system applies significant performance pressure and expectational bombardment at a time in our lives when it is needed the least.

Before moving on, I have listed several questions that came up continuously while researching this book. The answers were collected from data bots and previous questionnaires.

Should kids have recreational and physical education time?

YES

Should kids be graded on their recreation and physical education time?

NO

Should kids be allowed to strive for trackable achievements in all areas?

YES

Should kids have time to express themselves through art, music, and culture?

<u>*YES*</u>

Should artistic activities be graded?

<u>*NO*</u>

Should the child be allowed to complete projects and achievements to provide a sense of accomplishment and self-confidence?

<u>*YES*</u>

Is competition ok?

<u>*Yes, given that it is healthy & fair competition.*</u>

Should kids have structure & schedules?

<u>*Yes, life has structure.*</u>

Should children have 4 hours of homework after school?

No, *if the education process were more efficient, further study would be called progress. A student should be able to choose what to do with their personal time.*

Should we be worried about the happiness of our citizens?

Yes! *Recent data driven studies which considered happiness, life balance, and personal growth have shown that we are currently on the wrong path to fulfillment.*

Part 3: Kids Need Structure, Freedom, and Love

Often heard argument:
"The parents should be teaching these kids about life, love, and the pursuit of happiness."

In a perfect world, there would be merit to the previous statement. In the real world, we live in an economy that generally requires both parents to work an average of 50+ hours per week on top of their assumed responsibilities at home. If the parents commute, contribute to their community, or have educational requirements, there is no time left for anything else. It has become apparent that the fracturing of the family unit can be directly linked to a lack of work-life balance in society. The expectation for success has become so toxic and unattainable that it has caused an unspoken mental health crisis in the United States.

Due to ever-hastening wealth consolidation, a vast majority of society is left with the same odds for success you would find in a lottery disclosure. Success is no longer just about working hard, it is about knowing the right people to help you along, or just being plain lucky. Because 99% are set up for failure out of the gate, our entire planet is awash with people blaming themselves for their perceived inability to be everything to everyone, everywhere, all at once. As humans, we project our inner pain onto society creating a cycle of blame which enables war, apathy, and discord as a side-effect.

The education system <u>can</u> fill the gap currently left by societies expectation of adults.

Here's a quick visual breakdown of Maslow's 5 levels of individual needs that apply to everyone.

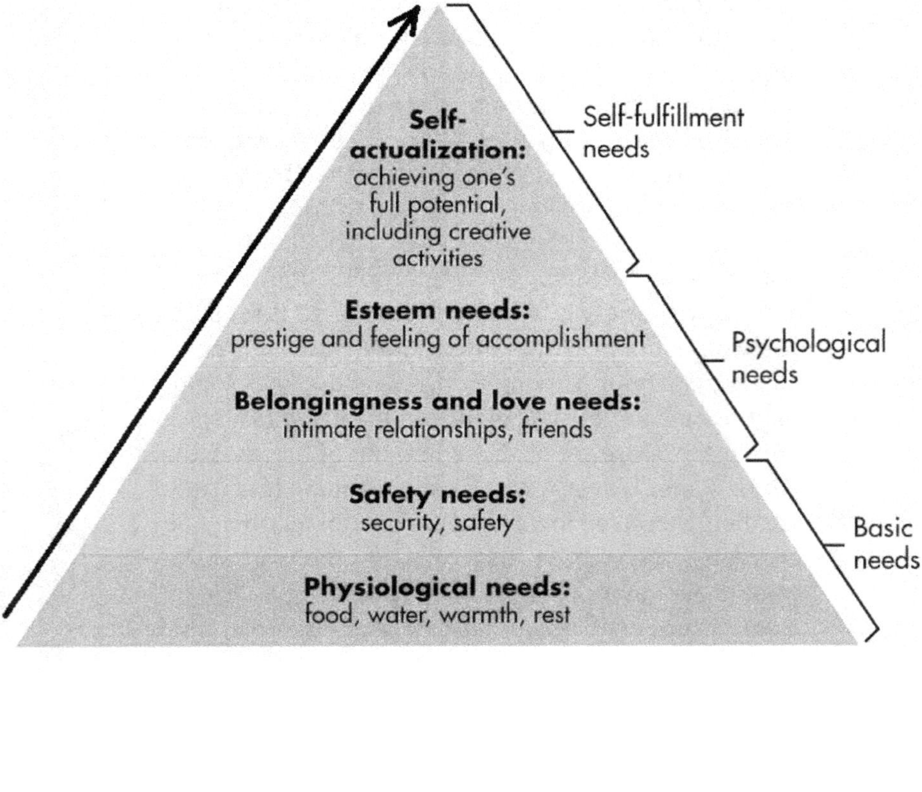

Sense of Identity and Self Esteem

Developing a personal identity, bolstering your strengths, and challenging your own weaknesses is what separates our species from the wild. Without knowledge of self, you can never truly know another person, nor hope to succeed in social aspects of your life.

Accomplishments & Projects

The rush of emotions, adrenaline, and accomplishment when completing a monumental task is difficult to describe.   Achievement and the experiences surrounding it define who we are from that moment forward. Achievement makes us infinitely stronger, certain that if we apply ourselves and work cohesively, we can accomplish anything.

In service of others, we must recognize that accomplishment is the biggest gift a person can give to their self-esteem next to self-acceptance. We must encourage participation and achievement for the greater good.

Sadly, many people currently go their entire lives without ever knowing true achievement.

Civic Involvement & Teamwork

To accomplish the truly monumental tasks we must come together as a unified force.

Being part of a team provides a sense of belonging, fulfillment, and importance. We learn from one another, find new friendships, and realize there is strength in numbers. Working with others on projects that directly improve our communities will foster long-lasting relationships and a sense of pride in who you are, and where you come from.

Health & Fitness

We must take care of ourselves by exercising regularly, drinking clean water, and eating the right foods. When regular exercise and proper nutrition are adopted, our energy level and cognitive abilities skyrocket.

Comprehension of what a healthy lifestyle truly is will go a long way in lowering societal health costs and improve overall quality of life. There is much truth to be found in the old adage "being healthy just feels better".

Optimistic Guidance & Leadership

True Leadership is not about the accumulation of wealth or power. True leadership seeks to achieve the stated goal whilst also seeing to the growth of its' participants. A great leader stomps out corruption and moral ambiguity in every action. Most of all, a great leader is thoughtful in every action and able to see beyond the immediate.
If we want to create truly great leaders to guide us into tomorrow, we need to foster their wisdom and growth today. Great leaders are not born, they are made.

Clarity & Emotional Intelligence

Learning to take a moment of consideration when a difficult problem presents itself is an indicator of true wisdom. As individuals, we must seek to gracefully endure the curveballs life throws at us. Self-control is a learned discipline, and enduring adversity with dignity takes practice. Developing our ability to be thoughtful, considerate, and practical is imperative.

Knowledge & Information
Knowledge^3 = Power

*In our society there will always be
certain individuals that covet power
and wealth above all else.*
Over the ages, especially the dark ones, it was
commonly known amongst royalty that If you wish
to prevent others from competing with your
dynasty, the easiest way to do so is by limiting
education. Restricting the knowledge of a populace
by meticulously shaping the flow and availability of
information to suit your agenda isn't a new idea.
The information age has not slowed these
occurrences of abuse. Instead, our digital
revolution has exponentiated both the practice of
and negative effects gleaned from this disgraceful
pattern.

*There is no honor to be found in
preventing another person from
achieving greatness in pursuit of
your own mediocrity.*
As the free market has proven, competition spurs
innovation. When the playing field is level,
companies must consistently push forward, fueling
the growth of humanity. Conversely, when
knowledge or methodologies are restricted and
held hostage, it only serves to delay advancement
and decelerate innovation.

*All knowledge must be shared for
consideration.*

Every university and government study should be accessible via a single integrated portal. If a global system was implemented, research and study data in its raw form can be re-evaluated and used where the content is relevant. Creation of a universal results & knowledge matrix could save us from tons of redundant work.

Adventure & Curiosity Fulfillment

Humanity is at its' best when venturing into the unknown. An unexplored horizon captures the imagination, invigorates the mind, and provides a sense of meaningful purpose. While mindless repetition of a skill or process may eventually lend mastery, it does not enable broad understanding. Our education system should consistently beckon us outside our comfort zone. We must foster an embrace of change mentality in our citizens and squash the fear-mongering that prevents modernization. If we place an "ever forward" ideology at the center of our societal focus, humanity will live like galactic royalty.

People should be able to live their lives freely, experience different perspectives, and make their own determinations about what "is".

Self-Expression & Creativity

Just let it out.

Many of the incredible ideas people have go unspoken, unrealized, and disappear as quickly as they materialized. It is a tragedy that billions do not have the knowledge or access to bring their ideas to life. Those without opportunity do not aggregate a network of knowledgeable companions earned from a long life of projects and successes. We need to foster intellectual communication and organically manifest tomorrow's ideas and improvements. We must encourage the beautiful chaos of our universe to be interpreted by diverse minds everywhere.

That idea, emotion, or flame of creativity that has been burning in your mind.

Let it out.

Perhaps this expression of creativity benefits only the one expressing it, or maybe it changes the way all of society experiences the future.

We haven't generated much data on early childhood development with alternative types of education, but given what we do have, we can make a few generic observations:

1. The education and scheduling needs of a person change as they age.
2. When we're young, we need more time for creativity and adventure.
3. As we age, we need to be able to focus our energies on personal and group achievements.
4. Guidance and structure should be heaviest in the early years with a lessening of restrictions as we age.
5. Progressive freedoms help ensure that children develop independent behaviors and ingrains the ability to conduct life without outside support or interference.
6. The younger we are, the more quickly we get bored.

If we build a system that grows with the individual, no one will have to experience classroom "downtime" ever again. All we need do is scrap the old system and start the new one tomorrow, right? Ok so maybe it's not quite that easy, but it's close.

How do we replace the system currently being used?

As citizens, we must provide the concept, formulation, and implementation procedures in a ready to go platform. With a grassroots effort and effective follow-through, this would be a huge political win for any administration.

Part 4: The Knowledge Tree

We all learn in different ways, and at different speeds.

To achieve our objective, we need a system that will:

- Allow an individual to progress according to their ability, needs, and interests.
- Supercharge the absorption rate of covered material and progress attained.
- Utilize standardized implementation procedures for classes and data.
- Provide professionals and students the tools to create new modules and constantly update data.
- Encourage continuing education throughout life.
- Have an achievement and reward structure that improves the social framework.
- Provide (at minimum) content for the 4 major learning styles. (Doers, Watchers, Thinkers, Reflectors)
- Create a system that can be implemented worldwide within current budgets.

The task seems difficult, but we can easily make it happen if we understand the who, how, and why of each individual's needs. To that end, let's learn a little more about knowledge absorption and learning types before we move ahead.

<u>Learning Types</u>
"Do-ers"

  Doers learn best with hands on experience and are the first to dive into any activity. A doer will learn from making mistakes and adjustments on the fly. In their natural environment, a doer is often found running directly from one task to another with very little downtime. This learning type seeks completion of tasks as quickly and efficiently as possible. A dominant doer personality is generally extremely energetic and can sometimes make other learning types anxious. Because of their dash-ahead mentality, the current education system represents a special kind of daily hell for a Doer.
  Doers are not generally interested in deep details or speculative musing on the 'why' of an activity. Doers will adopt what works best and disregard the rest. If you are a person that enjoys sitting in deep mental reflection prior to activity engagement, you will have a very difficult time keeping the attention of a doer.

Watchers

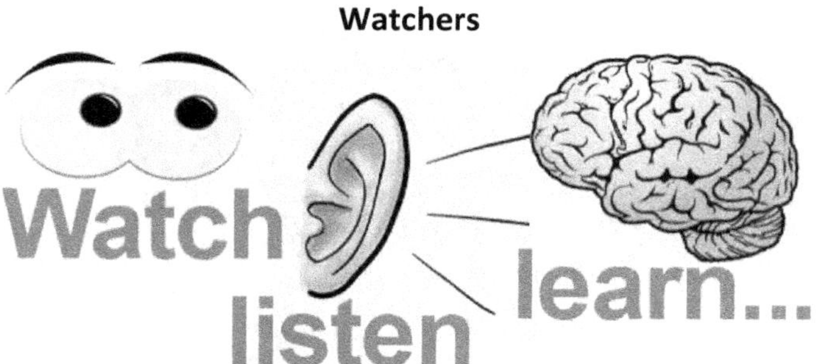

Watchers observe, note, and document each process to ensure they understand all steps before acting. A watcher considers all perspectives and possible outcomes often utilizing simulations and trials to find the best course of action. Expect a watcher to be the last to dive into a project.

To offset their lethargic participation upfront, a watcher will execute exactly as procedure dictates once involved.   This learning type exhibits patience in learning, and exceptional judgment in complex situations. A watcher can be a powerful ally in keeping a company, and their operations compliant. Watchers can be appointed as documentarians thanks to their innate attention to detail.

"Any fool can know. The point is to understand."
— ***Albert Einstein***

Thinkers

Thinkers are logical and analytical. They are planners, and followers of plans.

- Why does it work?
- How does it work?
- Where is the documentation?
-

The previous are all questions asked by a thinker. Thinkers will gladly help you review a mountain of data in search of an elusive answer. This learning type asks a lot of questions, benefits greatly from FAQ guides, and cherishes professional mentoring. Thinkers have a need to understand the big picture and have no use for hypothesis or gut suggestions.

Reflectors

Reflectors love a good story and excel as storyboard or UX researchers. This learning type represents the "people-people" of the world. Reflectors utilize perception and intuition to relate to others on a deep level. You can expect reflectors to be generally open-minded and sensitive people, showing genuine interested in your perspective, and those of everyone else.

A reflector is a weaver and conduit
for the "global story."

An interesting thing to note about learning types is that an individual usually displays 2 or more of the above. It is the identification and exploitation of their dominant type that should be of central focus during early education. Secondary learning types provide educators a fall back method if the initial content delivery attempts are ineffective.

Now that we know a little more about the different learning types, we can begin to visualize how we can effectively deliver focused content to our intended audience!

The Tree

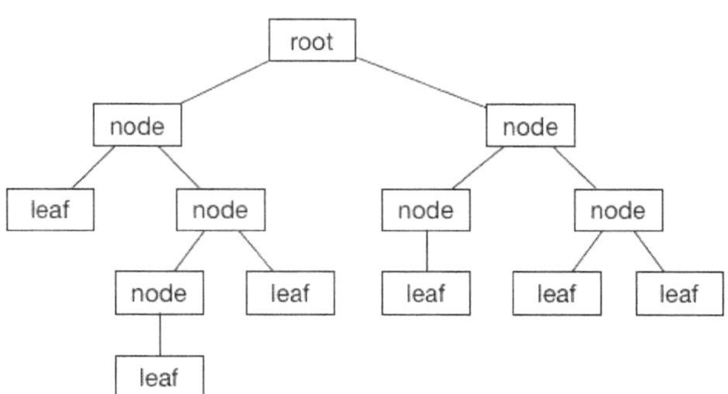

To truly explain this idea root to flower, we are going to need a tree for our data structure. A tree will help visualize the idea and allow for easier planning, development, and implementation.

Early on, the knowledge growth path is linear and heavily structured. Like a sapling, we must nurture, protect, and provide support for our children whilst also allowing freedom to grow. Because much of the later achievement is self-motivated, we must ensure that structure and importance of duty be instilled during the early phase of a child's life. Once the foundation is strong, the student should be free to branch out wherever they like, limited only by their interests and ability. Standardized educational paths assist in breaking down knowledge, expectations, achievements, and the resources necessary to present them in a digestible portion.

The best way to eat a five-pound hamburger will always be one bite at a time.

Roots (Basic Education)

The stated goal of the Roots phase should be to provide the basic education necessary to convey and understand module knowledge. Put more simply, a student needs to learn how to learn.

The Roots Phase should include nodes such as:
- ✓ Reading
- ✓ Writing
- ✓ Arithmetic
- ✓ Pattern & object recognition
- ✓ Communication
- ✓ Basic problem-solving
- ✓ Basic critical-thinking
- ✓ Basic citizenship
- ✓ Hygiene & self-care
- ✓ Basic team-work
- ✓ Motor skill development
- ✓ Self-governance
- ✓ Creative expression
- ✓ Basic technology usage

During early childhood development, attention spans can be very short. Children must be moved frequently to new activities in hopes of consistently renewing engagement. In early childhood education, learning and play must be intertwined into each activity.

Both micro and macro focused data should be collected on the outcomes and productivity of each activity to assist in global planning of future content.

The long-term performance analysis can also be used to personalize learning plans as students progress.

A side note: Children should have plenty of time to be children and run amuck.

All Roots topics will be tied together into a verification point that all citizens should seek completion of. Roots is the only education level which must be passed in its entirety prior to proceeding. There should be no "automatic graduation" of this phase, even in cases of special needs. As uncomfortable a topic as it may be, expectations must remain equal for everyone with no exception. The base purpose of this system is to ensure that everyone be allowed to go as far as they are able, and that all achievements hold the same weight.

Target completion for Roots Curriculum should be around 8 years old.

It is VITAL to this program that no age conditions or restraints be placed on ANY level.
If the pre-requisite content has been completed and understood, **age should not limit achievement.**

Trunk

Once a student attains the abilities to convey, grasp, and interact with the data being presented to them, they should move onto a curriculum more suitable for their skill level.

The Trunk utilizes the mental nutrition gained from the Roots and provides a wide foundation for continuing growth. A few of the primary differences regarding this phase:

- There must be a clear path to achievement, but students are allowed some flexibility and self-determination in curriculum choices.
- It is important to provide a sense of personal freedom during the self-discovery phase while maintaining scheduling structure. "Flexible Freedom" will assist in self-regulation development.
- Data extrapolated from efforts in this phase can be utilized to determine strengths and weaknesses. Additionally, the child will normally begin their lean toward a specialty area which can be helpful for upcoming decisions.

<u>A list of Trunk Primary Node examples</u>

Math

Having grasped basic numbers and operations like addition and subtraction, the student should move from intermediate operations like fractions/multiplication/division all the way up through what is now called Pre-Algebra.

Science

The most important aspect of this node is to provide students with an understanding of what science is, how it is quantified, and the processes involved. Once the Roots are strong, basic physics, natural science, biology, and chemistry should be learned. This phase should be capped off with scientific projects and "experiences".

Civics

In the Roots phase, your child learned the basics of interacting with others. In this phase, focus is placed more on civic responsibility, understanding government functions, and local issues. It is very important that a strong understanding of the challenges and questions facing humanity are conveyed.

Technology

In the trunk phase, students go beyond simple user interaction via introduction to the basics of electronics and computer science. Modules in this phase would include things like intro to coding, animation, user interface design, basic hardware, software use, and online awareness.

Instead of producing "users", our education system of the future will produce creators.

Critical & Creative Thought

Some individuals are born with an inclination toward creative or critical thinking. In most cases, this inherent ability is a one or the other proposition because the fundamental aspects of the mentalities are different. In our world, there are individuals who are primarily left brained, and those who are right brained. By encouraging the development of innovative thought combined with the ability to scrutinize new ideas, we can bring balance to the consideration processes of all.

Communications

What is an idea if you lack the ability to convey it? Nothing.
Advanced communication, structure, and grammar practices should all be components of this node. We should convey the concepts of data and extrapolation, imparting the ability to make informed declarations to others.

Social Science

The true goal of this phase is for a student to begin the path toward self-worth, autodidactic achievement, and confidence. Society can provide the gift of a "wisdom bridge" to self-understanding by laying bare the experiences of others. When we teach the knowledge obtained from Social Science, we can provide a sense of the inherent communal struggle, which by proxy provides a sense of belonging and purpose. On the path to self-awareness, it is nice to know that you are not alone.

Teambuilding

Learning how to be a reliable and effective team member is vital to future achievement. Our near-future economy will be one of perpetual projects pushing us further into prosperity. Instead of panic, disarray, and struggle, we will respond to global and local issues with hordes of proven people who have all necessary skills to get the job done.

Team projects, sports, challenges, and studies should be constant and ever-changing. Students should be encouraged to actively participate in two or more of major teambuilding efforts per year. Integration of team projects into the curriculum helps ensure that students enjoy regular achievement throughout life. This maintains a level of self-confidence necessary for success.

There should not be achievement created for the sake of achievement. Participation ribbons for those who didn't participate, and universal rewards for those who do not deserve them must become a thing of the past.

Rewarding lethargy, failure, and non-participation can be more detrimental to long-term individual mental health than we previously realized. False praise creates a "minimum to get by" mentality in our society and has devastating consequences to personal expectations. Those who experience unfounded accolades throughout life end up having an undeserved and unhealthy sense of entitlement as adults. Entitlement generally leads to an individual being a drain on both family and society as they age.

Teams will always be as strong as their weakest link.

Personal Health

The ability of the body to provide proper nutrition and resource flow to the brain has a massive effect on cognitive function and problem solving. Learning how to properly care for our bodies, and achieve fitness without injury, is important to our quality of life. Healthy bodies start with regular exercise and planned regimen rotation to prevent over-exertion. Finding the motivation to keep up an exercise routine can be difficult at times, so it is important that a student be able to choose their activities and routines freely. Some individuals prefer to run while kicking a soccer ball downfield, while others prefer earbuds and a woodland path. Whatever your preference, do the work it takes to keep your body in tip-top shape.

Food Knowledge is another HUGE subject that currently does not get the attention it needs. Student curriculums should teach about where food comes from, how it is created, and how to prepare delicious meals from basic ingredients. If children are taught early about the concepts of production, processing, and renewal, we will all live healthier lives.

Personal Growth

The only person who can pull me down is myself, and I'm not going to let myself pull me down anymore. —
C. JoyBell C.

Einstein once said that by accepting our limits, we are able to go beyond them. When an individual can accept and love themselves for exactly who they are, they beckon true happiness. A state of genuine well-being empowers the individual to achieve great things and inspires all who come into contact.

Achievement allows us to cast aside the shackles of self-doubt.

Personal Interests & Projects

Expanding your abilities through the exploration of hobbies, crafts, and conventions leads to life changing experiences.

People should passionately pursue a plethora of personal paths. Over time, exposure to multiple ways of considering, executing, and most importantly, completing projects will have an enormous effect on both the student and society. The end result will be a planet full of capable project managers, who double as complicit and powerful participants in any endeavor.

Imagine a world full of capable, determined, and passionate people.

Now imagine how incredible our combined effort can make the future.

➢ Completion of the Trunk Phase is required before moving on to the Branch Phase.
➢ You do not need to complete all offered content in the Trunk Phase.
➢ A specified amount of Elective Interest Nodes and Achievement Points will be required.
➢ The target age for completion of the Trunk Phase is around 12.

Branch Phase

*If we prevent a butterfly from
opening its wings, it will always
remain a caterpillar.*

From the Branch Phase onward, the student is
provided with much more freedom to determine their
path. The general age for the Branch Phase is 12-16
years old. As a society, we recognize that the teen
years are generally the most challenging in a student's
life, for a myriad of reasons. Flexibility in scheduling
and freedom to choose one's own path will hopefully
quell the rebellious nature inherent in all of us.

Keep Calm, Accomplish Feats, and Celebrate Life

Early adulthood is when we grasp emotional intellect,
social capability, and true team functionality. During the
Branch Phase, a student will begin to exhibit the facets
of "true wisdom" and the ability to see beyond the
seen. It is during the branch phase that most students
will develop their convictions, social triggers, and
political passions. Because of this, the Learning Center
must constantly seek to protect Branch Phase students
from institutional bias. The individual must feel free to
explore, experience, and become who they are meant

to be. Then, and only then, will you output a truly "well-rounded" adult.

While freedom to explore is
important, of equal importance is
the need for continuing structure
and a growth in expectations.

As citizens, we have responsibilities to ourselves and one another. People depend on us to do our part, and by doing so, we ensure a better quality of life for all. Only through communal trust and reliance upon one another can we accomplish the truly incredible feats that lie ahead. Each citizen must be able to recognize their value and place in society.

Steady participation in group activities, builds, and intellectual endeavors imparts integrity and leadership. Diverse project participation teaches us how to utilize the resources available and manage expectations for follow through. Group participation, struggles, and occasional failures teach us how to deal with the conflicts inherent in our nature, enabling us to seek graceful resolutions. Just as students desperately need to experience achievement, so too must they experience failure. Reverence for the light cannot exist without acknowledgment of the dark.

During the Branch Phase, roughly 15% of an individual's waking hours will be spent with other students doing project or sports activities. Unlike previous phases, the majority of the Branch Phase is spent alone, focused intently on individual knowledge aggregation. If we embrace this new approach, it can make an awkward time in everyone's lives much less so.

The Branch phase will take an individual through what is currently a 2-year college degree in the United States.

Curriculum elements will provide a strong intermediate understanding of all core subjects and provide knowledge bridges to specialization leaves(advanced), and flowers (mastery).

 While some specific content is required to complete this phase, most credits will come from student attention to specific focus areas. An overall achievement point and node threshold will be the determining factor for completion.

Important considerations for this phase

- Many classes included in this phase are required for later specialization.
- Specialization preferences should be considered as a student plans their curriculum.
- Students can continue to complete nodes from these phases at any time throughout their life.
- The concepts of enforced pre-requisite learning come into play.
- Once completed, credit remains even if modules change. (Credits Never Expire)
- Students have 100% control over their workflow
- Students must plan participation in regularly scheduled learning center activities for themselves. (Sign-up, add to calendar, attend)
- Projects and Participation are required for all specialties. The future will be one of "projects".
- Signing up for group classes and projects will cost Achievement Points.
- Sign Up Achievement points can be lost for failure to complete group and team projects. This makes a student personally invested.

- All sign up points are given back upon completion of an endeavor, along with the newly earned Achievement Points.
- No time limits or Achievement point penalties should be placed on personal academic projects to allow for flexibility in community demands.

Depending on the student's ability and drive, the completion age for this phase will normally be between 16-18 years of age. Once completed, the citizen should for all intents and purposes be considered an adult, responsible for their own well-being and future.

Upon Branch Phase completion, specialization 'Leaf' nodes can be embarked upon.

I want to provide a visual example of what a branch might look like in simplest terms. Forgive me for anything left out, or where the branches stop, but we only have so much room. I gave a Math, Science, and Technology branch example. Unlike most trees, these branches constantly re-intersect. Those nodes are checkpoints prior to moving onto more difficult content.

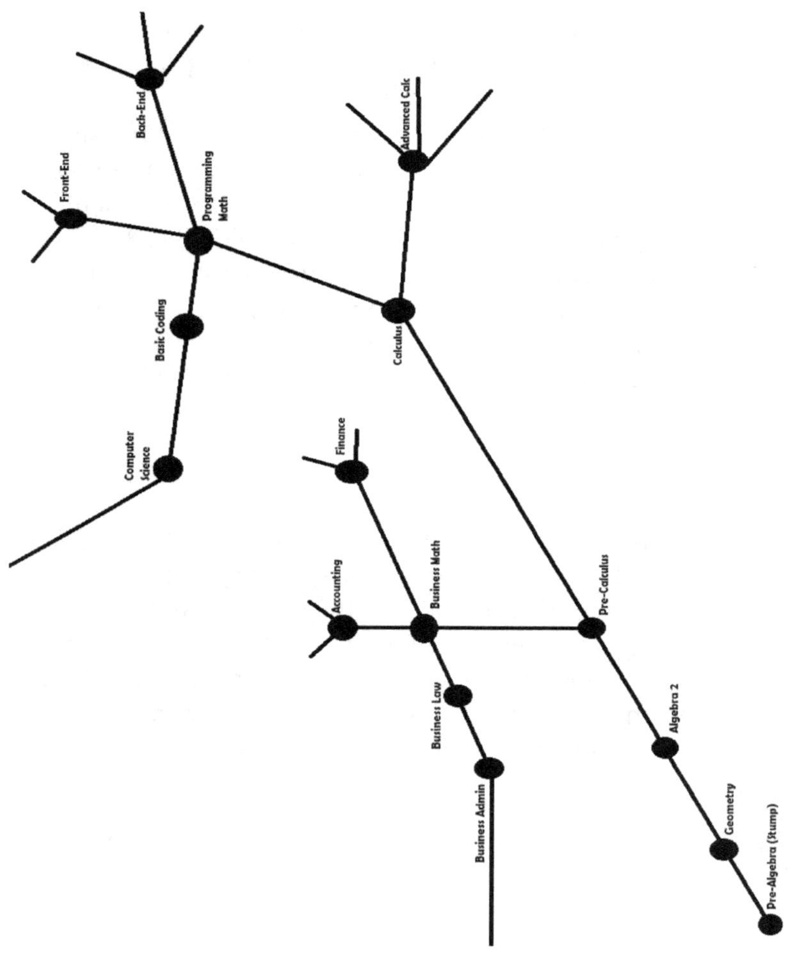

Back-End
Front-End
Programming Math
Advanced Calc
Basic Coding
Calculus
Computer Science
Finance
Accounting
Business Math
Pre-Calculus
Business Law
Business Admin
Algebra 2
Geometry
Pre-Algebra (Stump)

Professionals in each field should consistently come together and decide the most efficient and effective guidelines for achievement. Human understanding evolves every second, and our ability to convey accurate information must remain as agile and responsive as possible.

Outside interests, be they political or
private, must be shunned at all costs.
The only considerations tabled
should regard the effective delivery
of educational content.

A list of primary branches for this phase include
Math, Science, Technology, Civics, Government, Business, Economics, Artisan Skills, Strategy, Philosophy, and Life Skills.
A certain number of node points will be required from each primary branch, but limitations should not exist on which nodes specifically within the branch must be taken, aside from linear pre-requisite classes.

Our goal is to achieve a well-rounded
education which plays towards an
individual's strengths utilizing
technology, efficient functionality,
and universal access.

Quick side story: A close friend of mine hated math when we were younger. "I just don't understand why I would ever need it." he would say, referring to Algebra. The teacher we had in high school made the cartoon character Droopy look like a dynamic rock star by comparison. Using the term "dry" doesn't even come close to describing the experience. My buddy barely passed the class and felt confused about what he had learned. His negative experience in the class made him timid about mathematics and flatlined his interest.

Fast forward several years and my friend now loves Algebra and uses it every day. During college he had an incredible professor and was exposed to content that completely changed the way he thought about math. To be honest, my friend should have excelled at math his entire life. His lack of progress in the field wasn't due to a failure of intellect, nor was it a direct failure of the original instructor, it was due to a system failure in effective delivery of content.

> *We must provide content specific to each learning type for all educational nodes.*

Content examples include talks, lectures, video, hands on projects, exercises, live tutoring, games, and anything else deemed worthy as a teaching tool. By focusing all energy into these modules made for mass consumption, each option can be molded into an instructional masterpiece. Our educational content, like our technology, will get better and better over time. . Each update to the system or a module is indeed a step forward for all humanity. Our societal descendants will forever be freed from listening to the 800th regurgitation of textbook paragraphs by a brain-numbed victim of the system. Our instructors will evade the monotony of repeating lengthy lessons and be free to focus on facilitating personal and societal advancement.

Leaves

Leaves represent a Master's degree level understanding of a specific subject matter. Standard examples of leaves would be Statistics, Software Development, Particle Physics, and Artificial Intelligence.

Upon satisfaction of a leaf, the individual is considered "certified" on that subject matter and can be counted on to have problem solving and production ability within that field.

There is no limitation of age or how many leaves an individual can conquer in a lifetime. Counter to the philosophy of previous generations, it is important that the system encourage inter-disciplinary specialization. Mankind's global hivemind will grow exponentially if every citizen has multiple roles they can fill.

Leaves will craft the future directly and provide the output necessary to sustain the human organism. Leaves are leaders of tomorrow who focus ideas and energy to shape the future. As a bonus, If we effectively build our system, they will also be well-rounded, self-confident, and happy adults.

Flowers

*When left to grow freely, the cream
of the crop tends to rise to the top.*

Flowers represent the crowning achievement of our future education system. Society should revere, and be inspired by, these beacons of societal progress and achievement. Flowers are equivalent to our doctoral level individuals with a mastery of all given subject matter (leaves & modules) in their chosen branch.

*Only upon completion of all leaves
on the terminal branch would a
candidate be awarded a branch
flower.*

Flowers are recognized as leaders in their fields, and indeed, as leaders of humanity. Flowers should be tasked with the updating and implementation of all content in their branch on a global group scale.

Part 5: Is that a fact? No seriously, is it?

The web is a big place. Our hyper-connected households harbor our personal portals to an endless sea of information churning out at a rate that defies understanding. Our globally dispersed deluge of data diarrhea has created an ever-churning soup of improper keywording, algorithm pleasing fake news, and just enough pop-up ads to push you to your rage limit.

There must be a better way to get
the information we need.

The 4 Big questions for the next age of education are:
- ➤ How do we determine what is real, unbiased information?
- ➤ How do we define what is important to education and what is not?
- ➤ How do we ensure that from an education side of things, students are only exposed to relevant material and nothing else?
- ➤ How do you prevent a group of special interests from high-jacking the system for their own use?

These questions sound tough upon first reading, but we need not fear, the processes we follow to solve the above problems are very clear.

Step 1: Open Source/Hive Mind collect ideas for the guidelines around which the process will be created.

Step 2: Group, refine, and list processes.

Step 3: Open source/Hive Mind vote on final process lists. Each item must be voted upon individually.

Step 4: Create finalized list and universal standardized process with detailed explanations for each.

Step 5: Turn documentation over to UX & Design team for storyboarding, research, and wireframing.

Step 6: Security team identifies class, controller, and function naming conventions for development & source code implementation.

Step 7: Turn all documentation over to development team for implementation.

Step 8: Development team creates an opensource skeleton version of the build with instructions, needs, and a communication board for the global community.

Step 9: The global development community makes short work of the necessary functions and class designations.

Step 10: Completed code is submitted to the central team.

Step 11: The core team reviews the completed code for accuracy and security purposes before swapping the encrypted source code naming conventions.

Step 12: Code is saved into final build.

Step 13: Code reviewed by security team.

Step 14: Code goes beta for testing.

Step 15: Code goes live.

In simple terms, the process starts with the creation of a set of guidelines around which a standardized digital process will be based. Developers will create an app that allows for the submission and automatic processing of a new modules putting them on the path to implementation.

Once the process is in place, new modules can be created by anyone that has achieved the appropriate clearance levels. Once populated and ready for review, modules will be released to the public forums for debate, reference checking, and version editing. To avoid trolling and false submissions, an individual's real name will be assigned to the module submission as the author or contributor.

Upon satisfactory completion of the consideration process, a module will be pushed to the global system and achievement points allocated to the author(s) for their contribution to society.

As new modules are debated, improved, and approved by certified individuals all over the world, they will receive upvotes. When an upvote threshold for approval is reached, a finalized version of the module will be provided.

After certification, the prospect module moves up to implementation phase. During this phase the module is reviewed, finalized, and signed off on by flowers. Afterwards, the core team uploads the module to the secure servers for official use in the nodes. All certifications and upvotes are kept as public record.

#RealTalk Warning

Another aspect to be considered is outside influences which seek to distort or color the information being provided for their own benefit. It is my personal view that any individual seeking to control or manipulate the flow of information to the detriment of society should be viewed as a criminal in the future. I would additionally note that if an individual or group wishes to speculate, or maintain beliefs counter to current scientific understanding, they should always be free to do so. Previous statement now in place, I would put forward that devoid of scientific proof, these beliefs should never be made part of the education system curriculum.

<u>Which leads us to the absolute necessity of verifiable evidence.</u>

Verification methods can often be just as important as the claim in question. All sources for a given subject should be digitally linked and mapped. Raw study data should be made readily available within the nodes and modules via a separate data portal. Instant sourcing and raw data availability will help solve massive problems we currently experience involving publication bias in scientific studies. It is vitally important that all raw data collected be published. Raw Data and derived outcomes provide students with a deeper understanding of how conclusions are extrapolated and back the claims made. If you found the right answer, you should have no problem showing your work.

All topics should have links to their body of evidence within the same node as a reference.

If no body of evidence exists on a given subject, studies should be planned to provide the necessary evidence. One of the most powerful aspects of this system will be the ability to plan, approve, and execute necessary studies within the student base. Real-world studies and data generation should occur regularly, and in tandem with pursuit of further understanding.

Truth is as truth does.

Takeaways from this part should include the following:

- Included theories, ideas, beliefs, and assumptions should be **clearly** marked, labeled, and placed in a completely different view format from proven content.
- There can be no possibility of user error or confusion between fact and theory.
- Separation and identification of proven vs unproven/disproven information is crucial.
- No deviation can be made from the standardized public process for information inclusion.
- If you want it taught to our children as part of the primary curriculum, we simply ask that you prove your theory to be true with hard evidence.

An entire section of the curriculum should be devoted to exploration, adventure, and the formation of one's own beliefs and ideology. As discussed earlier, individuality and unique viewpoints are extremely important to societal progress and should not be governed.

A Learning Center is no place for religious or political dogma.

*People should have the right to
pursue happiness in the manner that
is right for them, given that it does
no harm to others.*

<u>Part 6 Achievements, Projects, and Gamification</u>

With each project completed, we gain new skills and heightened self-confidence. As time passes and our energy wanes, looking back over the personal works completed in your lifetime provides a sense of nostalgic validation. You know that you are a part of something truly special, and that a lifetime as a human, is a grand one indeed. Achievements will always stand to remind us of exactly what we are made of and how far we have come. Wouldn't it be nice if it was all saved somewhere other than our memory?

It is past projects that pave the way
for future achievement.

The idea of Achievement Points as an educational tool is brought to us thanks to the video gaming industry. Through the study of gamification, companies have been able to map what truly motivates us as individuals. Thanks to their extensive efforts, we now have a better understanding of what makes an activity fun, educational, and universally adaptive to social norms.

Everyone should focus on what they
are passionate about, and how it can
be used to improve society.

Have you ever gone into an office that just felt, different? Everyone within proximity is smiling, laughing, working, and eager to help. Every action seems to be coordinated, and every interaction genuine.

Scenes like this occur when amazing leadership meets passionate project teams. Now let's take it one step further and imagine a world full of groups like these!

Data and employee surveys over the past several years have shown that boring, monotonous corporate offices are going the way of the dinosaur. Life-chiseling vampiric work environments drain innovative enthusiasm, hamstring productivity, and stifle retention. The air in old school corporate environments is bereft of enthusiasm, leaving employees anxious, susceptible to depression, and prone to develop either self or externally abusive behaviors. In the modern era, if employees do not feel appreciated, nor valued as members of the team, they will lack sense of purpose and passion for what they do, and it will surely show.

Traditional Long-Term Employment
is no longer a thing.

Over the next 8 years (2019-2027), we will watch idly as automation takes over the manufacturing and logistics industries. Soon, only creative jobs requiring a human touch, individual projects not easily digitized, and technology jobs will remain.

If all the jobs are gone, what will we do with our time?

Projects.
Lots and lots of projects.
Mostly with teams, some alone.
Projects, projects, projects, and more projects.
An educated and agile project team will conquer almost anything thrown their way.

Gamification

Before I delve deeper into Gamification, I would like to comment on my own bias. The term Gamification and marketing theory behind it are, theory. However, the science behind specific aspects of that theory are solid, and proven by mountains of data. As I work my way through this explanation, I would ask that focus be maintained on the individual aspects plucked from the overall theory (the provable bits). As with many buzzwords in the technology sector, Gamification is a few proven principles wrapped in a web of marketing glitz, making it seem more complicated than it is.

So, what is Gamification?
Gamification includes the following "categories"
1. Challenge
2. Skill
3. User Engagement
4. Learning
5. Goals
6. Organizational Productivity
7. Reward
8. Achievement

Some organizations place these items in a specific or logical order, but we need a little of everything to make our system top-notch.

*It is the challenges we face that
define who we are.*

Everyone likes a challenge. We are attracted to the idea that if we push hard enough, we will receive a reward. Whether the reward is affection, admiration, monetary, or pride there will always be one amongst us that rises to meet opportunity.

The Learning Centers can use data, statistics, and creativity to make sure we all push it to the limit.

*We are all unique, and that is
powerful.*

Each of us is born with unique skills that we learn to leverage as we grow older. Future educational institutions must consider the development of a student's primary skillsets and abilities instead of ignoring them. If we play our cards right, we can spawn entire generations of people who have pushed their abilities to near super-human levels. Let us take advantage of what we can, to overcome what we can't.

User Engagement is a measurement of how a user interacts with a system, platform, item, or type of content. Data Scientists have been able to create incredible algorithms that collect, extrapolate, and provide preference data on users enabling better strategic targeting. Implementation of user engagement tools within our education system will make for a streamlined and efficient user experience.

If you didn't learn something new,
you probably weren't doing it right.

The universe is an endless sea of mystery and knowledge waiting to be understood. It is only by venturing into the unknown that we are free to discover new facts, ideas, and society changing experiences.

Each new day must be an unstoppable expansion of personal happiness, ability, and knowledge. As a society, we can experience unbridled mental growth, expression, and creativity sparking a human spirit revolution. Together, we can create a beautiful story for all instead of just some.

Everyone deserves the opportunity
to rise to their full potential.

The true difference between those
who succeed, and those who fail, is
the effective planning and regular
achievement of goals.

Goal setting is another important aspect of long-term educational participation.   It is important that reward from the system not be the only mechanism this ideology relies on for success. An individual must learn to value and reward themselves for achievements. Going even further beyond self-adulation, individuals must be taught to see the macro-view impact that their efforts create. Each of us makes the world a better place with every success we achieve.

<u>We must learn that it is ok to be proud of ourselves.</u>

You are only as strong as your production bottleneck.

Definition of organizational productivity: A measure of a given system, production method, machine, person, or process and its ability to efficiently create a product or technology.

As a hive mind we must address as many of the foreseeable problems during inception of the project as possible. Through careful planning of our future education system, we can avoid being overloaded with reactionary response issues. If we are prudent, the path to educational success can be clear from the beginning and the problems few. A strong start will allow us to focus on and solve the major issues that inevitably come up, with lightning speed.

Immediately after live implementation, Learning Centers will begin to measure operational efficiency, collect data on anomalies, and identify opportunities for improvement.

Reward

*The greatest rewards are not
material, we forgot that for a while,
but we are remembering again.*

The last 200 years have witnessed a whirlwind of progress, population growth, and quality of life improvement. Within a single generation, the pace of our global growth has gone exponential thanks to computer science and the internet. It is my _belief_ that mankind will look back on the span of years from 1994-2044 as the most rapid expansion of humanity toward being an interstellar species.

When my children are having children, people will be able to spend much of their time seeking happiness. Automation will take care of the production, cleaning, and labor necessary for human survival. All citizens will be strengthened by the comfort in knowing they are a part of something incredible. Each of us will once again know the power of being present in the moment. Our intense interpersonal relationships will seem to stop the flow of time just like they used to.

We can have it all.

Achievement

*Material rewards and emotions
wither over time, but true
achievement will be remembered
forever.*

As I said before, achievements define who we are, how we behave, and our expectations going forward. Think of all the ideas you had with friends over the years that were never executed because we lacked the knowledge of "how".

All students should be inspired to:

Do something awesome.

Make something awesome.

Be someone awesome.

And be proud of it.

The above categories are what guide the implementation of Gamification principles into any system. Code jocks and developers need to have a deeper understanding of the mathematical theory behind this idea, but for everyone else, this is the gist of Gamification.

The primary idea to take away from this section is that we should build value into **both** the individual and the system. This is done by goalsetting, measurement, and recognition of achievement.

<u>Part 7 Universal Documentation and Verification</u>

Designing an education system that will be beneficial to all learning types is a monumental task unto itself, but it is just the tip of the iceberg. To truly succeed, we need a system that is efficient, straight-forward, secure, and easy to maintain.

In further consideration of efficiency, learning types, and framework, how do we:

1. Ensure that credit is given where credit is due?
2. Provide instant verification of individual achievement?
3. Ensure security of data and personal information?
4. Create a system that is consistent in content, presentation, and performance expectation.

To solve these issues, we will need to utilize a combination of local Learning Centers and verification nodes across the world.

- ✓ Multi-node systems provide endless backups and verification points in the event an abnormality occurs.
- ✓ System abuse or hacking can be minimized by eliminating non-secure access points.
- ✓ Module (education) fraud can be prevented by using fingerprint scanners as part of the system.
- ✓ Personalized and secure technology kits should be provided to every citizen for educational use.

Universal documentation standards and practices have been in place for a long time. An organization called ISO, International Organization for Standardization, has been assisting in the development of processes for the commercial and industrial sectors since the mid-twentieth century. It is their mission to facilitate communication of organizations worldwide, but they aren't as data driven as they could be. Currently, I know of no leading worldwide effort to create standardization of digital data for open-source global cross-utilization. This is most likely because no one wants to share data, unless it benefits them. While information mongering may be of strategic importance in the competitive private sector, the same rationale does not mesh with the true purposes behind education.

 A large part of this educational revolution depends on the creation of a standardized research and documentation system that will play nice with an online delivery platform.   We then combine those two platforms into a secure user portal for students.   The portal view would be served by hardware hubs in every country and voila! A digital education system. Ok, it's not quite that easy, but it is well within the realm of our current capabilities.

But, How?

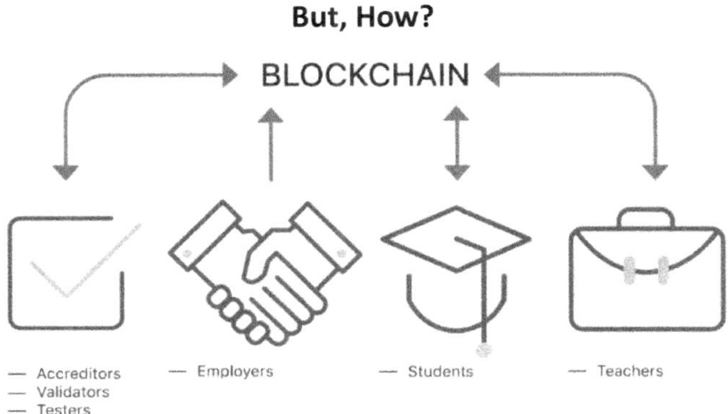

Network hubs would utilize blockchain style verification and updating methods to prevent tampering, loss of data, and ensure accuracy. By separating the content controllers and servers from the database of records, we can encrypt each phase of the process. This will also allow us to segregate secure and non-secure requests. A tertiary public record reporting system controller could then be created to instantly verify an individual's progress and accomplishments, without risking a breach of personal rights.

While short in explanation, this part of the process is the most difficult to achieve. It will require worldwide consensus and effort toward the creation and implementation of a truly universal system.

IN THE FUTURE, NO ONE WILL TELL YOUR STORY, IT WILL TELL ITSELF.

Part 8: The Student Kits

At the age of 4 a child is ready to receive their Initial Student Kit (ISK), and to attend the half-day Learning Center program. The half-day program is designed to assist in the adaptation of the student to life at the L.C.

The initial student kit includes:

- ✓ Unbreakable & Waterproof tablet with simple and direct-action interface (no outside access). Tablet also has a built-in beacon if lost.
- ✓ Special pack that holds their tablet securely in a hard case. Release button for tablet should be on front of backpack.
- ✓ Water Bag and leak-proof straw to fit into hard compartment on bottom of pack.
- ✓ Secure ID and locator badge

The ISK will have interactive games and educational content specially created for consumption during this critical time in a child's development. It will also provide instructions, directions, and act as a digital babysitter for the child. Total control, guidance, and interaction will take precedent until around age 8.

Once the student is ready to accept responsibility for it, the "Student Kit" can be requested. This kit will include everything a student needs to succeed in our digital world. The Learning Centers will act as a disbursement hub and repair station for all technology necessary for success. In the event of a required upgrade or issue, most of the work will be handled by students. This guided action will be a part of technology student's hands on learning. Hardware & Technology specialists will release standardized instructional procedures and boom! Instant global repair techs.

It is important that Student Kits be brand new for each citizen. There should be no hand-me-downs because hopefully, students will use them their entire lives. Occasionally, items will need replaced, and that will be part of our cost consideration shortly. Interestingly though, items will not need replaced as often as we have grown accustomed to. Most upgrades are caused by bad software and planned obsolescence in the private sector. This is part of the profitability matrix for all electronics manufacturers. It is important that a public facility with no outside interests build and program these kits. It is just as important to eliminate the fluff in the equipment as it is the content.

The Student Kit Should Include:

- ✓ V.R. Standalone Headset
- ✓ Set of Hand Controls w/ Built in Fingerprint Scanner
- ✓ Encrypted Laptop w/Fingerprint Scanner
- ✓ Noise-Cancelling Headphones
- ✓ Custom Protection Case

When a student advances to the point where effective education requires more processing power, such as software development, computational science, visual production, etc.; they will be granted an additional system in a desktop format for personal use. This system will also require similar security measures.

Let's break down each piece of the kit a little more and explain the purpose behind the items.

A.R. Standalone Headset & Controls

Augmented reality interactive hardware has rocketed into the spotlight over the last few years. New environments are being created daily, and the uses for this technology seem unending. A few examples of possible applications are pilot training, surgery instruction, machine maintenance, and pretty much every other type of program you can imagine.

The headset and hand controls should function as a single unit. The left thumb should be inserted into a fingerprint sensor that will take verification at the beginning and end of a module. Thumbprint recognition should not be taken continuously, because movement during the session could throw a functionality error. If there is a lull in activity or input, an additional measure could be an intermittent scan requirement. Each headset must also have its own blockchain id codes. One code would be a public id used to identify the equipment itself, the other a secure and encrypted private code known only to the student and the system. This private code should never be shared. As a third layer of security, a personal password which can only be set at a learning center terminal will be required to login.

Encrypted Laptop

The personalized and encrypted laptop is essentially a replica of the functionality built into the headset. A fingerprint scanner and secure system connection are necessary for use. All equipment in the kit should be able to communicate directly with the headset for cross-productivity.

The laptop should have a built-in motion sensing camera for participation in interactive classes and training modules. The built-in camera should have a sliding manual lens cover to protect the privacy of the student when not in use.

You may be asking yourself, why do I need both?

1. User input will most likely remain fastest via keyboard, until the full realization of direct neural input.
2. Digitized on-the-job training is more effective when you can simulate reality.
3. Longer independent battery life can be achieved via laptop, allowing the student freedom of travel.
4. Certain types of digital hands-on tests will only be achievable by use of A.R.
5. Usage of both technologies allows for more possibilities in content delivery.

All pieces of equipment should include a theft proof beacon to prevent misuse.

Private network connections will no longer be necessary within the next few years. I feel confident that given the opportunity, a fair partnership could be forged to deliver secure education communication capability to all.

Part 9: Digital Infrastructure

We will touch on Learning Centers soon, but first I would like to talk about digital infrastructure. To function properly, our new education system would require secure data servers. We need to be able to store student data, courses, and software controllers (preferably on different servers,) in a way that is accessible and connected to the rest of the global verification network. It is important that these hubs are service-localized to maximize performance and minimize wait times. Speed of service, accurate reporting, and automatic updating are imperative in our system of the future.

In addition to the standard user load, we must also strive to automate as many of the workloads associated with education as possible. Additional processing power and communication bandwidth will be required to carry out these tasks. Automation lowers demand on manpower and serves to prevent tampering and errors.

All servers should be housed inside the Learning Centers. A small portion of each facility should be designated as secure, temperature-controlled vaults for vital technologies. Limited access and strict monitoring will protect each node from interference. In the event an abnormality occurs, the node can be quarantined before the next global update.

Software matters naught without the hardware to serve it. Thankfully, the cost of building servers is lower than ever. The search engine giant Google recently paid $110,000 per server rack with 80 nodes (servers). This represents a massive drop in price thanks to automation and scale of production improvements. We can expect digital infrastructure prices to continue to drop as large racks begin being replaced by multi-qubit quantum systems over the next few decades.

Given current computing capabilities, covering the populated portions of the world with fast and efficient access would require approximately 1500 data centers. The total population served would determine exactly how many nodes are necessary in each center. We would need on average 10 of these racks per hub system, based on the current number of students served.

When we take the necessary nodes and multiply it by current costs, the amount comes out to about 1.15 billion dollars. Each server rack would also need replaced every 10 years or so. Over a period of 40 years, this would be approximately **4.6 billion dollars**. We will use this figure later as we figure out our final costs for implementation.

Aside from Learning Centers, the other major infrastructure cost we must consider is access. How will our individual students communicate securely with the global network, no matter where they are?   The most likely solution is a partnership with a global provider of network access. If a flat rate of say, **$100 per year**, per student could be negotiated, the company would provide profit for shareholders, and the taxpayers would get a solid deal.

If we build it, the rest will come. Society will always be building some new campus or complex, the real focus needs to be on building something universal, accessible, and culturally indifferent.

Part 10: Student Transportation

In rural areas especially, it can be half of the battle for people to get to and from school or work each day. How do we build a student transportation system that is efficient, effective, and on-demand?

Self-driving cars, buses, and drones are already being tested worldwide. The technology is here, the acquired knowledge databases are growing, and the future is one of driverless cars. Level 5 vehicle autonomy is going to change everything. Society will no longer be bound to mindless driving activities and frustrating commutes. Technology can take us by land, air, or sea to wherever we please. Each day we produce electric semis, buses, and personal vehicles that go further, faster, and cost less to power than their gasoline counterparts.

The truth is, a world full of autonomous vehicles is a MUCH safer world. The elimination of human error coupled with the automation of traffic flow will virtually eliminate congestion and accidents. Learning efforts and personal relationships will be positively affected thanks to this newly found 'free-time' during commutes.

Pick up and drop off requests will be made via mobile app request.

If someone wises to travel during off-peak hours, or from a point inefficient for bus travel, a smaller personal autonomous vehicle (PAV) could be sent for retrieval. To protect the system from abuse, vehicles should only travel back and forth to their closest Learning Center. The only exception would be if a community decided to opt for a public transit system following the same guidelines, or for special events at outside locations.

Beacon pickup points should be no further than half a mile apart. At regular intervals, the system should automatically re-determine the shortest possible route. The automated routing system should also dynamically change based on whether a pickup request was made. Optimization and automation of a student transportation system will drastically lower costs and student delivery times.

The process would go something like this:

- User sends a pickup request
- Beacon System Receives Request
- System Sends Request to Automated Routing Control (ARC)
- ARC determines most efficient pickup and adds request to pick-up queue for vehicle
- Vehicle adapts new route and sends confirmation back to ARC
- ARC sends notification of success to Beacon System
- Beacon sends confirmation and arrival eta to User

As data from usage statistics is refined, we can further maximize our impact by using predictive algorithms. Systems should be put in place to prevent misuse or requesting and then not being there when the transport arrives. The end-result will be everyone getting where they need to be, much faster.

Big talk but how do we pay for it?

As much as I hate to say it, school bus drivers will be a thing of the past, but so will many other jobs over the next 40 years due to automation. Truck Drivers, Surgeons, Factory Workers, Fast Food Staff, and nearly every other non-creative/non-technical job will become careers of yesteryear. Don't worry, I am sure we can find a way to fill in our extra time.

The budgeting for student transportation in the United States is difficult to pinpoint because so many different departments must be considered. A collection of all that information would be a book unto itself! To make it easier, we will isolate and eliminate the Department of Education Transportation Budget with overall savings derived from adoption of the new system.

Part of the educational curriculum in the civics branch will certify certain citizens as monitors. Monitors are well prepared and will know what to do in case of emergency or danger. In cases of special need, a student can be paired with a willing monitor via the app.

In general, Citizen Monitors can be counted on by society to be helpful in times of need. To entice participation, monitors receive Achievement Points for their assistance of others. If a bus is required to accommodate the number of pickup requests made, it is safe to assume that at least one of the passengers will be a responsible peer or monitor. In addition to civilian assistance, digital monitoring from a control center should also be utilized. Control Center monitors should have the ability to stop a bus, open all doors, lockdown a bus, and summon authorities if necessary. This is an important note for developers to consider as it will require additional encryption and communication security.

At the end of the day, transportation all boils down to efficiency and cost. How do we achieve the highest service levels possible while maintaining the lowest cost per student average we can? Let us delve into the numbers just a bit so we can begin to gain perspective on the issue.

The average school bus driver in the United States currently makes $33,037 per year and there are 381,410 employed nationwide. That comes to 12,600,642,170 or 12.6 billion. If the buses are automated, we will be saving the majority of these funds. Roughly 30% would still be needed for special needs transportation helpers. That would leave us with about 8.2 billion per year in savings just from manpower changes alone.

 The upfront price of electric buses will be about the same as their diesel counterparts within the next 5 years thanks to incredible advances in the output and longevity of battery technology. This will bring the cost to around 150-350k depending on the size of the bus and included options. We will call the median about 250k since that is the price point of electric buses currently in late-stage development.

As discussed earlier, some of the fleet will also be made up of smaller, and much cheaper, personal vehicles. Because the Learning Center is utilized at different times, locations, and frequencies, we must embrace the most efficient means of conveyance in every scenario. Cost per transport should be a built-in calculation within the app. Though the difference may be pennies per consideration, the year-end accumulation result will be astounding.

As the sophistication of the fleet increases, and more effective air-space management tools become available, automated flying drones could also be added.

Exploration into this travel method should proceed slowly to ensure the safety of all.

The operational efficiency of the system will allow it to shoulder a much heavier transportation burden without increasing the overall fleet cost. Adoptive use of the system will also significantly decrease surface traffic, especially in urban and campus areas. The above improvements will mean fewer people spend time stuck in traffic, which will increase overall societal efficiency by proxy. Operational improvements and standardization are long overdue in education.   For other sectors like business and manufacturing, similar upgrades have shown as much as a 400% increase in overall output.

We could also talk about Hyperloops and vacuum tube magnetic levitating trains, but let's save it for another time.

Great strides have been made involving battery supercharging methods that cut recharge rates to as little as 10% of the current time. These systems are already being tested and production scaling is being planned as I write this book. As mass production of these flash charging nodes increases, the viability of an all-electric fleet becomes further solidified.

The long-standing argument spouted by supporters of combustion vehicles has been that electric cars were more expensive, and the batteries lacked longevity. Electric vehicle technology has long since put those arguments to rest. Only the uneducated still find themselves swayed by the snake oil

****RANT WARNING****

As the days go by, the continued fight by the petroleum industry and auto makers has become difficult to watch. Currently, there is no consideration given in the bulk of the auto industry for what the customer wants, or what will help improve the planet. The only consideration for these organizations is how they can give consumers the least amount of improvement possible, while charging the most they can get away with. Sadly, these despicable practices are not limited to just one company, it affects all combustion-centric organizations. Every auto manufacturer in the U.S. market before Tesla has at some point entered into an industry agreement that put them under the thumb of fossil fuel distributors. Industry strong-arming forces manufacturers into a catch-22 where they can't evolve technology, because it would hurt fuel profits.

What a world we live in.

People die each day because of health issues directly related to vehicle pollution. Marine life suffers as we endlessly plunge into the earth for more oil. We suffer because progress is not profitable, and our government legislators are paid off by lobbyists to discourage them from doing anything to protect our citizens. When a smart guy can build an electric car that costs 60k and it makes the world's leading gas supercar look like it has the acceleration of a lawnmower, it is hard to argue any benefit to gas engines even exists.
END RANT

A future transportation system should be planned as an all-electric vehicle fleet.

The annual fuel cost savings of electric over diesel school buses is approximately $8,000 per year per vehicle! There are currently 480,000 school buses in the United States alone. Multiplying savings rates with the number of buses yields a savings of about 3.84 billion!

*A bus that runs on electric instead of diesel saves about $150k in societal health care costs over its lifetime. We'll just call this an **epic** bonus!*

The expected lifespan of an active bus is about 10 years. Upkeep and Maintenance of electric buses is currently 60% of the cost when compared to Diesel Buses. The training required to effectively maintain an electric vehicle takes a fraction of the time diesel mechanics require. Gas engines are extremely complicated and have a mind-boggling amount of breakable moving parts. Electric vehicles on the other hand are MUCH simpler. Replacing a battery or drive motor is a relatively clean and painless process. Speaking of clean, electric vehicle mechanics don't have grease covered hands and the smell of chemicals emanating from their bodies at the end of each workday.

Thanks to mass production, demand, and automation, we can now produce vehicles and parts more efficiently than ever before. If we standardized the transportation vehicles and the support infrastructure worldwide, all necessary parts would be plentiful and easy to fulfill. If we achieve true blanket adoption, the eventual maintenance cost of the electric fleet would drop to a fraction (possibly as low as 25%) compared to diesel.

Current maintenance costs average about $5,500 per year, per diesel bus in operation. If we multiply $5,500 times the 480,000 buses, we get 2.64 billion. If we are saving 40% ($3,300py), it would represent about 1,056,000,000 or 1.056 billion in savings off the current budget.

We can make this happen for less than we spend now!

Part 11: Learning Centers, Testing, and Teaching

*Learning Centers will be the heart of
the education system of the future.*

What exactly is a Learning Center?

1. A place for people of all ages to attend live seminars, talks, discussions, and information sessions.
2. A supervised testing facility used to prove comprehension by both traditional and/or direct application means.
3. Daycare & early education facility
4. Public make-space for individual and group projects.
5. Laboratory facility for testing and study.
6. A data and server storage center.
7. A place for team sports and community activities.
8. Administration and repair facility.

9. A place of comfort, safety, idea-sharing, and acceptance for all.
10. Community agricultural and cultural center.
11. Citizen preparedness center
12. Personal health & fitness facilities
13. Basic healthcare facility and clinic

Talks, Discussions, and Information Sessions

When information is delivered effectively and en-masse, it can change the world. Such is the power of TED (Ted.com). These online talks, and others like them, have propelled global understanding forward. On-demand access to diverse sets of information explained by the foremost experts in a given field cannot be matched by any brick and mortar institution. It is the ability to have the best of the best anywhere, in any place.

As new technologies emerge,
students and faculty can educate
their entire communities on a given
subject with one well written
module.

Learning Centers should become a hub for discussing issues, theories, and best courses of action. Societal decisions can be made by consensus on a micro and macro scale. If we create a population with solid understanding of scientific process, that consistently engages in theoretical debate, we will be limitless as a species.

Instead of relentlessly competing against one another for scraps from the table, we can work together as one. Cooperation can lead to communities so strong, nothing can shake them.

Supervised Testing and Procedures

Even with the benefit of thumbprint recognition, people will still find ways to 'cheat' the system. Parent fed answers, deep web answer keys, and cheat sheets will pop up for nodes and modules. Human beings are a clever and curious species. It should always be assumed by those charged with administrating our education system that a certain level of attempted tampering will occur.

To guard against undeserved achievement, Learning Centers will act as a checkpoint for knowledge.

Testing methods should take many forms.

Modules, nodes, and skills can be tested using book knowledge, practical application, project completion, complex problem solving, live presentation, or any other form deemed valid by the experts in a field. Advanced subjects and processes should use a combination of the above methods to confirm a thorough understanding of subject materials. In the event a student has trouble with a type of testing, they can opt for another type if available. Preferably, at LEAST 2 testing types would be provided for each node.

- A Module is made up of "Cells" of specific information, exercises, and sample questions for research purposes.
- Module tests should include information from cells in that module only.
- Node tests should include questions from all completed modules within the node itself.
- Leaf tests cover all completed knowledge in the nodes to which they are attached.
- Flower exams cover all Leaves on their terminal branch

Benchmark quizzes within the modules will prepare students for the expectations of the test itself. Quiz grades should not matter, aside from that a passing score must be obtained in each module within a node prior to Node Examination. Quizzes can be taken as many times as is necessary, and serve only as a practice for the exam. Module quizzes can be very long and detailed because they also serve as the 'homework' content within a module. Projects necessary for completion of a node should be included as a module for tracking & achievement purposes.

A Safe Space

- Learning Centers will be safe spaces.
- All public spaces should be monitored.
- Bathroom spaces should be private use.
- Everyone should take responsibility for the public space, and safety of others.

People should be free to express ideas, so long as it does not disrupt the education of others.

Your thumbprint and passcode will grant access to education facilities at the Learning Center. Controlled access provides accountability, zone security, and prevents people from wandering into areas where they could be hurt or injured. Children can be kept in a secure wing of the Learning Center away from the general education facilities. This age-appropriate segregation is for the benefit of all, and the reasons are many.

As a student moves forward in their education, they will gain more access and usage over the facility assets.

Compartmentalized access and digital verification techniques encourage an innate sense of individual pride. The access itself is a constant reminder of prior accomplishment, and a level of trust earned from society. We humans tend to feel better when a sense of belonging and accomplishment is achieved. Even sweeter is the victory if the sense of belonging is somehow "special" or "limited".

Beyond the self-adulation, a significant difference in the care given to equipment and facilities is experienced when access is limited to qualified professionals and students.

No more back to school shopping

Thumbprint validation should be used for material and asset dispensation. When a student needs something for a project, they simply check it out of the system with no interruption or wait times. The processes need to be made as simple as possible while providing the accountability and service levels required. Over the past 2 decades, these types of improvements have been all the rage for private businesses. One day, an auto manufacturer figured out that improvement equals profitability, and boom went the dynamite. Supply chain automation and process improvement should not be limited to production facilities. We can update our education centers to be just as agile in fulfillment and operation.

A better quality of life, for everyone.

Orphans and children in state custody should not suffer, nor be afforded fewer opportunities than their peers. If a dorm is included near the Learning Centers, these children could enjoy a much higher quality of life and self-determination. Planned proximity can cut costs and provide centralized access to necessary services like mentor counseling.

Daycare & Early Education

Until around age 8, children require <u>CONSTANT</u> supervision and guidance. Age 3-8 is the time in children's lives where they require the most structure in their daily activities. Every moment during this period should be carefully cultivated and continuously improved.

With strategic planning we can make sure children learn everything they need to know and have tons of fun doing it.

MakeSpace

I have personally witnessed the power of a well-equipped makespace. The skilled application of artisan and creative technology skills is just as important as the science behind them. We live in a time where a robot can build anything you tell it to, but you need to "create" the action. Regardless of age, people should be exposed to the methods and machinery behind production. When the children of the future become adults, there should be no obstacles between what they dream up, and what can be made reality.

Equipment power modules should be controlled by the same access verification systems as the doors. For example, a student would need to complete a safety module, training modules, and test prior to using a CNC router. Tinkerers and class participants will rack up certifications, knowledge, and further societal understanding all at the same time!

Learn. Do. Teach. Learn More.

Lab Facilities

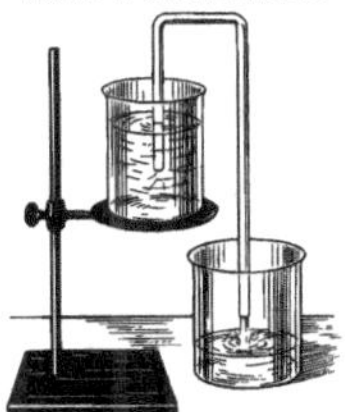

Usage of lab facilities for projects, curriculum, and knowledge studies should be coordinated via the student portal. Digital project management and standardized workflow should be instituted for proper filing and allocation of material assets. A properly devised project portal can double as the mechanism by which data and results are collected, processed, and shared.

Data Center

We talked about the data servers a little earlier. Data center servers would run from the secure heart of the Learning Center. Data centers will guarantee near instant service of content without bogging down external bandwidth with local requests. The data center network, and it's blockchain reporting structure, are vital.

Community Activities & Recreation

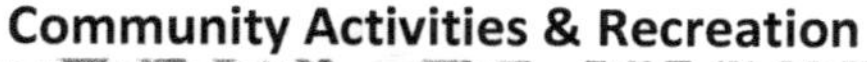

Friday night football, yoga in the park, and jazz under the stars will always be moments in life that we cherish. Centralized activities within the Learning Center should serve to bring a community together in fellowship and cultural appreciation. Learning Centers will become a place for non-religious & non-political interest groups to gather, form clubs, and execute projects. Diverse offerings could see a student attending a JavaScript coding meetup right after Judo class without leaving the campus. Centralized activities encourage people of all ages to come together and help one another fill in the information gaps in development and learning.

Like any community activity, the objective is simply to get people to come together.

Basic Healthcare Clinic

Injuries happen, yearly physicals must occur, and students need to learn about healthcare industry processes. A small on-site clinic can help provide basic student healthcare needs for non-emergency cases.

Administration, Security, & Repair Facilities

*Stuff breaks, decisions must be
made, and sometimes people act like
animals.*

Learning Centers would need an administrative staff on-site similar to today, but their duties would completely change.

Maintenance, scheduling and allocation

All scheduling of building updates, repairs, and facility improvements would be submitted via digital workflow.

Universal building layouts = universal upgrades

Automatic updates, upgrades, and rollouts should occur at regular intervals, and in all areas. Rural and urban areas should not suffer lack of access nor upgrades due to lack of local funding. Standardized implementation procedures and budgets should be provided for the communities to execute updates as they are approved.

Universal Consensus = Universal Consent

Learning Center policies should be decided via public consensus. No promises of private allocation should be made without public approval.

*In all cases and all times,
corruption should be actively
sought out and eradicated. It is the
scourge by which all others suffer.*

Administrative staff responsibilities include:
1. Reporting injury, damage, or behavioral incidents
2. Reporting abnormal wear or machine breakage requiring immediate attention.
3. Registration and enrollment of new students into the system
4. Providing Guidance Counseling
5. Conducting initial tours and orientation
6. Submitting requests, reporting errors, and confirming results
7. Assisting those in need
8. Leadership in the event of catastrophe
9. Care for children

The administrative team for an entire Learning Center should not be that large. If processes and scheduling are done effectively, a small, passionate, and agile team can handle these responsibilities.

*Security and safety are always a
concern. As a society we must
attempt to prevent any incident of
harm to self or others.*

Restricting access without authorization, coupled with location-based accountability, go a VERY long way in keeping a building secure. People are generally on their best behavior when they know they are being watched. Digital Assistant nodes should be placed in each room to help students, broadcast alerts, and receive vocal calls for help. Panic buttons should also be in every room. Students should **ALL** receive civic and basic response training, adding to the readiness level in case of emergency.

Learning Centers could be open from 5am-10pm each day, but would need to be closed during the overnight hours for the following reasons:

1. It discourages people from excessive study and work.
2. Allows for thorough, nightly security checks including infrared.
3. Provides time for readying and uploading of data updates throughout the global system.
4. Charging and cleaning of public transportation vehicles.
5. Allow cleaning bots and mechanical processes to occur without risk of human interaction or injury.
6. Oxidizing, ultraviolet, and chemical disinfection of all areas in the Learning Center

In the event of an emergency, exit routes should automatically allow for freedom of movement.

During all non-emergency times, check-in scans should be used. In the aftermath of an emergency, all students and staff should re-verify immediately after restoration of normal operations.

Custodial care within Learning Centers will be done primarily by AI machinery and sterilization procedures. Automation will eliminate a bulk of the tedious work necessary for staff. Standard maintenance, cleaning, and supervising of the A.I. equipment would be the trade-off. For specialized cleaning jobs that cannot be automated, a human touch may still be necessary. Harmony in function and effort between human and machine will give staff more time to ensure cleanliness, order, and proper functionality of all Learning Center facilities.

Repairs and routine maintenance on machinery, parts, and internal operational functions will be executed by a team of mechanical engineers. Learning Centers will boast an electric fleet, a brigade of mechanized sanitation workers, a heap of unique machinery, and near endless opportunity for expansion of knowledge. For the true engineer at heart, it is a haven of variety, offering exposure to many kinds of technology. Senior Engineers could teach apprentices as they work on tasks, providing a much earlier hands-on understanding for future colleagues.

All processes for the maintenance and repair of equipment contained in a Learning Center should be documented, digitized, and standardized. If standardized documentation does not exist, it should be created and globally shared. In the event of equipment malfunction or repair, information regarding the issue and solution should be documented, organized, and shared. Thorough documentation and data tracking will assist in identifying systemic problems and to expedite repairs prior to catastrophic events.

Cleanliness and order should be maintained by students through a combined use of 5S principles and equipment sensors. Each area should have a standardized layout, and equipment should be returned to its proper place prior to departure.

Sensors and digital assistant reminders will help a lot!

So, what is 5S?

5S is a Six-Sigma method used in manufacturing and operations.

1. Sort
2. Set
3. Shine
4. Standardize
5. Sustain

<u>Sort</u>

1. Eliminate obstacles and unnecessary items.
2. Evaluate what is needed, and what is not.
3. Red-Tag area to place unnecessary items or those tagged for removal (including trash).
4. Regular supervisory check-ins
5. Regular re-evaluations of necessary equipment
6. Sort items by parts

Set

1. Arrange all items so they can be easily selected for use.
2. Arrange workspace in a way that tooling and equipment maintain proximity.
3. Place components according to frequency of use, the most often used being the closest.

Shine

1. Clean workplace regularly and spot clean after each use.
2. Use cleanup time as inspection time
3. Remove dirt, debris, and buildup from the area.

Standardize

1. Standardize and document best practices in the work area.
2. Maintain high standards in workplace organization at all times.
3. Everything in its place
4. Everything has standard and universal coding/colors.
5. Processes are digitally stored by job type.

Sustain

1. Do no harm
2. Follow 5S without being managed
3. Perform regular audits and improvement suggestions
4. Goal oriented process geared toward training
5. Constantly seek improvement and further efficiency.

*5S concepts and societal courtesy
should be included modules in the
Civics branch.*

Good habits are formed via submersion, expectation, and repetition. The tenants of cleanliness, healthy eating, and courtesy are all habits we adopt over our lives. When you get right down to the basics, 5S principles can be expanded into every aspect of human existence, and we will be better for it. People will litter less, smile more, and take pride in the communities they live in. It all starts with proper education and environment.

Agriculture

Understanding food science, growth techniques, and making smart choices when it comes to eating should have a much more important place in education than currently occupied. Society can use Learning Centers as a continuous effort front to educate the population on nutrition and agriculture. Studies and experiments leveraging growth data and successes can be shared worldwide. We can eliminate hunger by providing the knowledge necessary to supply the masses. By introducing the concepts of vertical gardening, drip timers, nutrient wicks, and staggered crops, we can produce most of the necessary food for the facility. On-site food production provides educational and fiscal benefits. Additionally, fresh food can be produced for the community year-round. Imagine a lush botanical garden in every community Learning Center that mostly maintains itself, with only minor human work involved. Indoor crops are protected from pests, airborne molds, rapid changes in weather, sulfuric rain, and virtually any time that growing conditions are not optimal. Learning Centers and the knowledge conveyed will eventually provide humanity with another line of defense against starvation.

Food Production and facility maintenance in the Learning Centers will provide the exact same data and experience necessary to cultivate food off-world. If we can learn to live and work in these self-sustaining systems, we will stand a much better chance of survival.

Imagine if starting tomorrow, families all over the world grew some of the food they need to survive. It would ease dependence on processed foods, make our population healthier, and give people pride in eating what they made. Imagine neighbors once again sharing their harvests with one another. Imagine a world without starvation.

Art

Expressions of ideas, emotions, and improvements all have their origin in artistic thought. A good friend of mine, we will call her Jo, always said that "The earth without art is just eh." I think she is spot on. Innovation, imagination, and futurism are what drive mankind forward. We must open ourselves wide to the wonders of the universe. The passion and satisfaction experienced in the moments of creation can reveal the truest forms of self.

*Expression of emotion through art
can help repair mental blocks or
trauma we experience during our
lives.*

Student's should learn to take a moment away from expectation to stop and draw the roses. A required component of significant achievement is found in artistic reflection. Not all achievement is statistical, nor is all beauty computer generated.

Citizen Preparedness Center

In many cases, it is not the disasters themselves that cause the most damage. Panic, disorder, and lack of leadership in times of catastrophy are what tend to cause the lasting harm. If citizens are prepared to assist one another in times of crisis, many injuries and casualties can be avoided. Our combined awareness will ensure community reactions are both swift and orderly.

Preparedness, survival, and first aid should all be part of the Civics branch.

Health & Fitness

Facilities for sports and exercise should be centrally located and accessible to the community. Swimming pools, gymnasiums, fields, and practice facilities should be on-site whenever possible. Children below age 12 should have their own separate exercise and play areas.

Transparency and Monitoring

Secrecy and privacy are rights we all share. I would never condone an action that was geared at stripping mankind of their privacy while in their own home or property.
Secrecy and Privacy in consideration of public facilities, shared spaces, and Learning Centers however, should be a thing of the past (excluding bathrooms). This is a topic I have spent way too much time debating over my life. Sufficed to say, I have yet to hear a reasonable argument concerning the benefit of secrecy or privacy in an educational environment. The bottom line is that if you require secrecy or privacy to carry out an action in a public facility such as a Learning Center, it is of the

highest likelihood that you are breaking the law, or something counter to societal interest.

*All information should be shared,
and all efforts documented. Data
will prevent us from repeating our
failures and create an inherent trust
in the system.*

Monitoring will protect everyone within the facility. If people wish to cause shenanigans, they can do it in the comfort of their own home, or somewhere goofing off is encouraged. At a Learning Center, people come to better themselves, and they should be allowed to do that, in peace.

Cost of Overhead

Generally, the best way to learn about something is to see it, use it, and find new applications for it. It is important that Learning Centers have machinery and technology readily available for use upon certification. Book knowledge alone will not suffice in the world of tomorrow. Practical application, standardized procedure, and adaptive evolution are the pathway to mastery. It is very important that the resources and equipment be current industry spec. Wasting time training children on technology that will not even be an afterthought in the private sector, holds little value. Learning Center technology planners should include basic tools, 3-D printers, lasers, production technologies, medical technologies, and pretty much everything else that will function to create our future. The certification process will ensure proper usage and maintenance of equipment owing to a sense of ownership in the community. After the Learning

Centers are completed, data can be used to determine machine usage, waste, and additional needs.

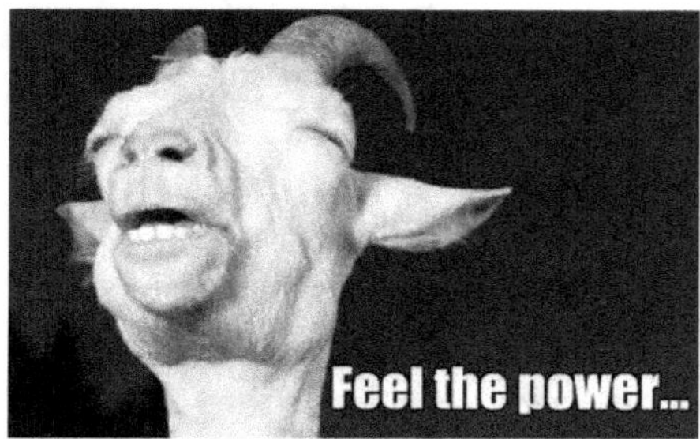

   In 2016, the United States spent 6 billion dollars on energy for schools. That's a big number.

   New Plan: Power for the Learning Center will be generated by renewable and self-contained technologies. Battery walls should be installed to assist in power availability and overall efficiency.

Publicly owned power creation, storage, and management are a lifeline for the community in the event the privatized power grid is compromised.

Energy redundancy would allow Learning Centers to provide a haven and rally point for citizens during grid outages, storms, or disasters.

   If multiple types of energy production are feasible in a given location, it only serves to provide additional educational opportunity. Local demands create specialists for the technologies driving energy production within the community itself. Learning Centers in Iceland would use geo-thermal energy, whereas a school on the western coast of Australia could easily generate wind and solar power. Remember, the way of the future is efficiency and optimization projects. Let's figure out the best solution for your community!

Newly constructed centers will utilize natural light from the sun where possible. Windows and sunshine are good for us, but can also pose hazards in excess, or during solar flares.

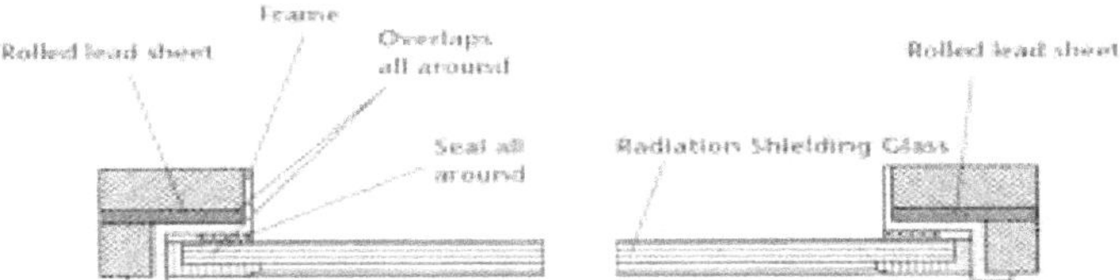

If we plan our facility using inset windows with automated sliding window shields, we can prevent most types of damage. Inset window designs also provide an effective test model for off-world applications. Ultraviolet and harmful radiation film filtering can protect citizens from damage due to exposure. Another large impact consideration project for each location is to have engineers adapt exterior colors to reflect or absorb heat. Everything that can be done to increase the efficiency of the facility and lower its environmental impact should be done, within reasonable consideration of human needs.

Learning Centers still need the grid.

Perhaps Learning Centers will evolve to be 100% self-sustaining, but for ease of implementation the system should be connected to both a sewer and power grid.

Rain water capture and usage in non-potable capacities for gardens, play fields, and landscaping would significantly reduce clean water usage. If the building is designed with capture, purification, and reuse of rain water in mind, the process of implementation is a snap. Students will also benefit from hands on exposure to the entire process of water refinement.

There is a lot more to discuss about the Learning Centers so the next few parts will break down the larger factors involved.

Part 12: Teachers & Administration

In this section, I would like to expand upon the idea of administrators, staff, and the people power necessary for success.

The administration of a Learning Center will be conducted by a team of proven specialists. Each department would consist of an administrator, junior administrator, team leaders, and specialists. The number of specialist teams required will be calculated by total population served.

Workflow and processes should be clear and well-documented for each administrator. The total number of people served should not affect the overall workload of the administrators themselves. It is important that the teams put in place function independent of direct supervision. Everyone will have a job to do, and if done correctly, there will be very few issues. When a major issue does arise, it can be quickly solved by coordinated effort.

We must always seek to foster the next generation of leaders. Additionally, much can be learned through communication between student and administrator. To that end, two part-time student assistants should be chosen each period to learn the responsibilities of administrative positions, and to gain hands on experience.

Internships provide an experience bridge if the student later wishes to enter public service. Sometimes, student internships like these also help us realize what we don't want to do the rest of our lives, and that can be just as valuable. We never truly know until we try.

Tutoring and group instruction will be handled mostly by advanced students, who earn achievement points for their assistance. Tutoring requests can be made by students on internal message boards and subsequently picked up by the willing tutor. Simple, effective, and a great way to encourage mentoring.

With 30 kids screaming in a classroom you aren't a teacher, you're a drill sergeant.

Dependence on direct instruction has already been drastically reduced due to large amounts of digital content available for each subject online. As we continue to develop, organize, and optimize our data presentation techniques, the demand will diminish even further. With such drastically reduced demand for focused instruction, finding an available tutor will be easy.

Administration positions should make the same amount in pay and benefits across the board. For example, all Jr. Administrators should receive the same pay no matter where they are located, or what team they are on.

Administrator salaries should be figured off the previous year's median household income, which in

2016 was $59,039. To stay ahead of inflation and make the position attractive, Administrators should receive +15% as a pay grade boost, where Jr. Administrators would receive a +10% adjustment above the median income. Team Leaders should be a target of about 7.5%. Specialists and Guardians should receive a 5% boost over previous year MHI. Pay rates should fluctuate yearly to adjust for variations in GDP. The last thing we want our educators to be worried about is how they will pay their family bills. They have worked too hard to have that kind of worry.

For full maps of staffing and other
nifty stuff, check out the website at
www.educationsolved.org

Central Planning

1. Central Planning is responsible for the communication, planning, and scheduling of all events at the Learning Center.
2. Allocation requests for resources and submission of finalized schedules to the global server will be authorized by this team.

Requests for events come to Central Planning via students, administrators, or central authority. Central Authority requests should be primarily used to announce breakthrough technologies and science reporting to the global community.

Financial reporting should be 100% digital, thus providing 100% accountability for funds. Utility fees, budgets, and resource allocations should be digitized upon creation and fed automatically into the overall budget. Humans should only verify entries and stage files for global upload.

Central Planning will also collect usage statistic information concerning equipment and facilities in the Learning Center. Verified and standardized reporting on usage will assist in rollouts of additional equipment and facilities on the macro scale.

Student Affairs

Student Affairs would be responsible for providing guidance throughout a student's education. The roles of guidance counselor, registrar, tour guide, and mentor are all within the realm of Student Affairs.

When people are first brought to the Learning Center, Student Affairs will get them registered in the database, fill out equipment allocation forms, and add their sign-in data to the system. Upon first visitation, parents will need to complete legal forms and documentation for their minor.

Age and achievement-specific counseling sessions should be scheduled throughout a student's life.

Sessions should be used to answer questions, resolve issues, and plan future path selections specific to the student's goals and desires.

In the event Achievement Points are earned outside the normal nodes, Student Affairs would make the request for approval and allocation to the network.

Science

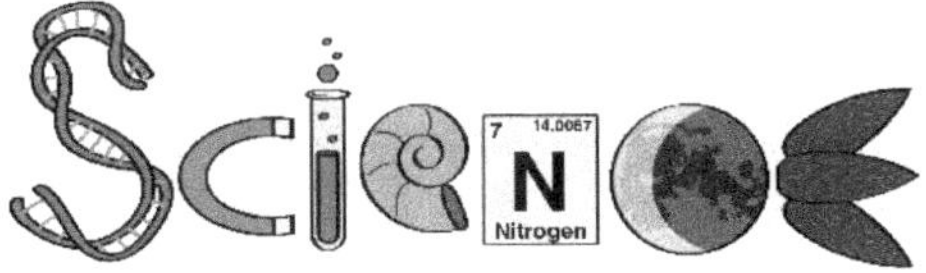

Healthcare, Physics, Biology, Chemistry, Astronomy, and many more fields of study all require unique labs, equipment, and knowledge. The management of these areas, and their resources, is a job unto itself. The Science Team will ensure their labs stand ready to educate the populace and provide the breakthroughs of tomorrow.

One of the greatest triumphs of the new system will be dynamic data creation and instant availability. Communal sharing of research data, conclusions, and methodologies will serve to more rapidly educate our populace. The exponential improvement is not limited to just our maturation rate as individuals though, it is a technology driven thruster strapped to the back of humanity. As our innovations become more complex, we can lean on this data to give us a kickstart on projects saving mountains of time. The world will be jaw-drop astounded by the amount of output achieved by macro community efforts.

The effect of having a truly educated population is something we as a species are yet to experience. Imagine the possibilities.

Technology & Development

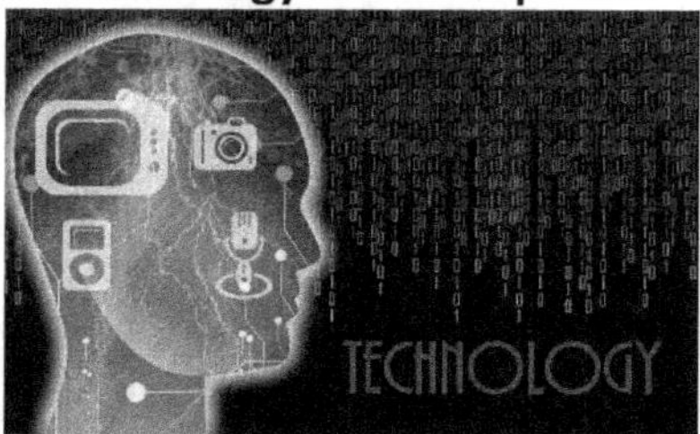

The technology team generates and enforces standardized procedures on electronics and advanced technology used in the Learning Center.

The tech teams will scan packets, install software, apply updates, and maintain restricted access equipment like servers. Technology teams are also in charge of replacements, recalls, and hotfixes for all technology related equipment used in the facility.

An agile technology team needs code jocks and network developers at the helm. Most repairs done on high-end equipment will require firmware or software interaction. Those who seek to serve their communities in this capacity need to be early-adopters with a thirst for seeking out bugs and weaknesses. This team should constantly conduct white-hat testing operations in hopes we will find issues before hackers do.

Central Planning and Technology teams must <u>both</u> approve server merge packets before being added to the global queue.

LC Ecosphere

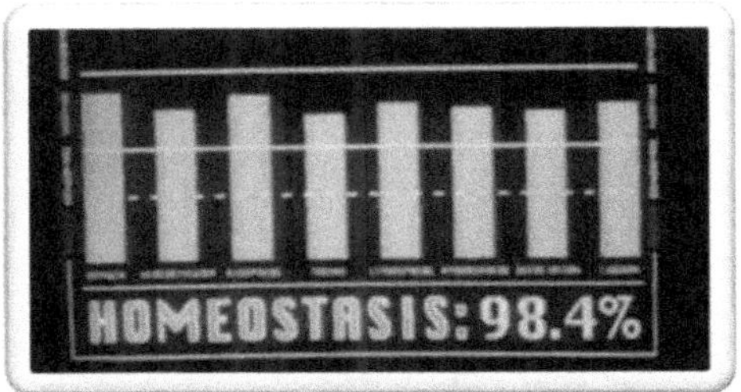

Maintaining a comfortable and clean learning environment for the masses is no small job. Ecosphere management oversees the coordination of deliveries, utilities, refuse removal, minor repairs, security, custodial services, maintenance, and everything else that keeps the facility moving.

Ecosphere teams work in coordination with other departments to plan and execute Learning Center improvements and activities. This team will be assisted by automation and provides the "muscle" necessary to move the planet forward. This department should take pride in providing a spotless environment. It is a proven fact that most people will go out of their way to keep an already clean environment from degrading. It is the theory that if you walk up to a clean sink with nothing in it, you are more likely to clean the dish you were about to leave. By impressing these standards upon our youth and making them part of the routine experience, we will find that cleanliness out in the community as well. This global effort toward a better environment will create one.

Math & Communication

Learning to effectively communicate thoughts, feelings, and ideas is central to the future of education. The Mathematics and Communications team will work to research and introduce new forms of content, see to proper vernacular representation, and train troupes of talented tongues ready to serve their nation and planet.

Math and Communication teams combine the practice of story-telling and user experience. They analyze and implement data collection and information standardization procedures. The Math & Communications team listens, interprets, and conveys. This team should represent a cross-section of individuals who have mastered communication between humans, technology, and the universe.

All Learning Center departments will find themselves somewhat reliant on the Math & Communication team for development of new modules and nodes for global distribution. Math & Communication teams also provide leadership and guidance for Learning Center projects.

Civics & Social Science

Learning about yourself, others, and how to work together to achieve the society of tomorrow is the task of the Civics and Social Science team. Society places a great responsibility on this team to forge well-informed, educated, and engaged citizens ready to face the challenges of the future.

C.S.S. teams are responsible for teaching students how to care for themselves and others. Citizens are prepared for emergencies, adult life, taught survival skills, safety, project facilitation, and provided a firm understanding of laws and government process by this team. Most importantly, this team will assist individuals in learning how to make educated decisions on the issues facing themselves and society. If we had a well-informed general population, the citizens could vote directly on issues and government size could be scaled back.

Assistance from C.S.S. may include grant writing, permit requests, government liaison work, and handling of student legal issues.

Child Services

Child Services will be the largest department at the Learning Center. Total employment will depend entirely on the number of children needing support. The Administrator would receive the same pay as outlined before. In cases of extremely large service populations, it is possible there would be up to 2 Jr Administrators. The Child Services Department would have several Team Leads to provide a communication and accountability point. There are many responsibilities to consider, and automation cannot fulfill certain aspects of child care.

Student to Teacher Ratio will vary by age group drastically. Children under 12 make up about 40% of our total active population and they must be supervised by more than one entity. Because children between 8 and 12 can somewhat self-police, they require a ratio of about 25:1. Children under age 8 require even more attention and are best kept in smaller groups of around 8:1. 40% of our sample school district's 2,960 students is 1,184 students. For ease of calculation, let's say half of each group are represented. For our 8-12year old group we have 567 students at a 25:1 ratio requiring 22.68 staff. Our younglings of 4-8 require an 16:1 equivalent to 35.43 staff members. In total, we know our example LC will need 58.11 staff dedicated to child education.

State fostered children would be assigned a team, much like a house in your favorite magic tale. They would remain on this team for projects and themed events throughout their education as a minor. When dealing with children who have been separated from their parents, it is just as important to provide a sense of belonging as it is to provide opportunity.

Safety is number 1, always. Children under the age of 12 should be required to wear an id badge that contains a tracking beacon while on LC grounds or transportation. This id badge would also serve as a geo-fenced alert should the young student accidentally wander off.

Guardianship

 Guardians manage the security of the children at the Learning Center and take steps necessary to keep them from harm. The Guardian working domain also extends to nearby dorm facilities as part of a total care system. Much of the facilities and living spaces will be under the surveillance team. At the age of around 8, the child should be given their own living space which is not monitored. Though small, it should provide opportunity for privacy and personalization. This is extremely important. It will provide foster children with a sense of control and self-determination that they otherwise are not afforded. For safety reasons, adults should never be alone with children in their personal space. In the event of emergency or child-endangerment, a team of at least 2 staff should assist, unless medical intervention necessitated immediate action. Through this method we can achieve a sense of freedom and security for all.
 Learning Center Guardians should either be an extension of, or replacement for, current child management programs. A program built this way would provide 100% assurance that no child is left behind due to circumstance.

Outdoor & Recreation

Safety, maintenance, and management of equipment, and children in outdoor environments, is the task given to Recreation Team members. The Outdoor & Recreation group helps students stay healthy, engaged, and away from danger. The amount of activities and facilities that can be packed onto a Learning Center campus is limited only by its geographic location and demand. Facilities should be constantly maintained, improved, and evolved.

A healthy mind requires a healthy body. It is one of the few things we can say with confidence about our reality. Let's do everything we can to help our communities stay fit.

As a note: The common play area for children should have a retractable covering for bad weather. It is very important to instill strict schedule adherence and discipline during this phase in life. With the help of a giant weatherproof roof, children can stick to the plan.

Sorry rainstorm, these kids need exercise.

Food & Custodial

Kids are **REALLY** messy. Maintaining a sanitary environment that fights back against the bugs brought by busy explorers is an important job. The truth is, we need to focus much more on sanitizing these environments than we do today. With recent news that hand sanitizers are making our children less healthy, and that exposure rates are increasing, it is overwhelming to consider the manpower necessary to keep us safe from infection. Thankfully, we have lots of automated help!

It would be silly to put so much effort toward health and not talk about the 800-pound gorilla in the room. No child should ever go hungry. This much we all agree on. But is feeding them unhealthy garbage any better? It simply delays the health issues for another period in life. Processed foods and sugars are causing a health crisis, particularly in the U.S. We can at least try to provide healthy food choices to our children early in life with hopes it will follow them as they age. Learning centers should provide cafeteria areas only children can access. These minor-specific cafés ensure that all children have access to proper nutrition and can also be extended to those living in the dormitory to fully meet their nutritional requirements.

Fulfillment

Fulfillment teams ensure that the resources necessary to teach and care for the children are readily available. This includes everything from apples to zippers and would extend to students in state care at the nearby dorm.

This team will most likely shrink over time as fulfillment practices are standardized and optimized. In the early stages of Learning Center operation, the Fulfillment Team should be slightly overstaffed. If the resources the system needs to function are not available, the system breaks down.

A closed and automated P.O. system will protect from abuse. Only vetted and approved vendors should be added to the system, and these vendors should be reviewed annually. All payments and activity should be made available for public scrutiny.

Artisan Skills

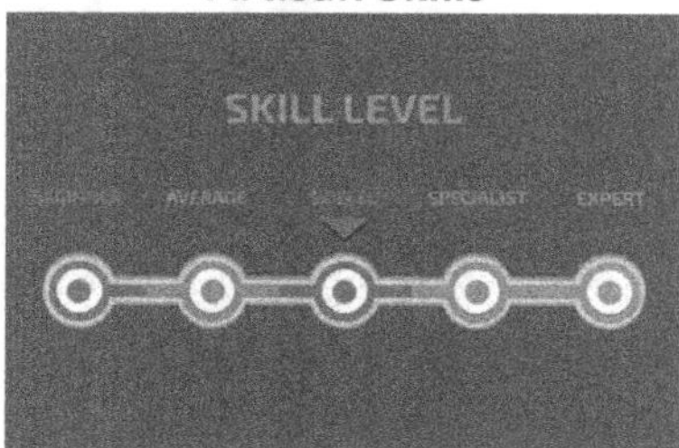

The administrative team for artisan skills will focus on the delivery of hands-on content and instruction. Organization and rotation of activities, experiments, and demonstrations should be the responsibility of the Artisan team. Acquiring skill sets from these areas is vital to implementation of ideas and theories later in life. I simply cannot stress enough the importance of this currently underrepresented area. Some of the skill areas that should be included (but are not limited to):

Electrician Residential (R) & Commercial (C), Plumbing (R&C), Millwrights, Mechanical Engineers, Riggers, Woodworking, Metal Working, Welding, Machinists, CNC/3D Programmers, Modeling, HVAC, Masonry, Construction Methods, Heavy Machinery, Robotics, Machine Learning, and much more!

Creativity and imagination will be the most powerful skills in the future. It would only stand to reason that we would need the skills necessary to make our ideas into reality.

Health & Fitness

Healthy Bodies + Healthy Foods = Healthy Minds

They say ignorance is no excuse for breaking the law, but somehow it is an excuse for torturing our bodies. Many of the health problems people have are directly related to nutritional and gut health. If our bodies are well-nourished and our bio-system balanced, the results are just noticeable, but powerful.

Smart-choices begin with education and self-discipline. If we instill the concepts of healthy eating, organic production methods, and schedule adherence into our citizenry, good health will become the norm, not the exception.

We need to make sure the offerings for fitness are diverse. Not only will this make the overall program more inclusive, it will also allow for individual experiential meandering. Variety is and will always be the spice of life. Pour it on.

Part 13: New facility planning

An idea is just an idea.

The framework we have created so far begets a model of our intended outcome. Now we must put our plan into action! Something concrete to build our dreams around. We need our first Learning Center.

I am not an architect. I am not a structural engineer. In this chapter I will attempt to provide an example of a Learning Center layout. Like all ideas contained in this book, and the book itself, we will evolve, one version at a time until the best concept is found. I will provide a place to start, building upon the incredible ideas of others.

In this section I will reference numbers pulled directly from statistics online. Because I live in the United States, and our system is as bloated as It gets, I will reference our numbers. This means that any country better managing its GDP allocations could implement with less overall difficulty.

Let's start collecting our numbers...

 Reference:

http://www.k12.wa.us/SchFacilities/pubdocs/OSPI-ESD112K-3CostStudy.pdf

MEDIAN SQUARE FEET PER STUDENT

	State Median (New & Existing)	2014 - 19th Annual New School Construction Report National Median	2015 - 20th Annual New School Construction Report National Median	2016 - 21st Annual New School Construction Report National Median	Average of the National Median of New School Construction Completed 2013 thru 2015
Elementary School	115	149.6	188	135.3	157.6
Middle School	148	173.3	173.4	180.1	175.6
High School	173	174.2	180	181.9	178.7
Skill Centers	138	N/A	N/A	N/A	N/A

From the above statistical data, we know about how much space we need per student served. Our Learning Center will serve people of all ages, on one campus, and that is an overall consideration we need to make.

Let's look at the standardized build budget for a consolidated school corporation comprised of 2 elementary, 1 middle, and 1 high school. This would serve a small sized town. The <u>average</u> size and budget look like this:

	Students	Sq. Ft	CP Sq.	Cost
Elementary School	624	84700	211.55	16200000
Elementary School	624	84700	211.55	16200000
Middle School	612	118500	246.96	26500000
High School	1100	173727	235.29	45000000
Total	2960	461627	226.33	103,900,000

Table Reference:
https://www.montgomerycountymd.gov/OLO/Resources/Files/2017%20Reports/OLO%20Report%202017-4%20New%20School%20Construction%20Costs.pdf
and
http://www.doe.virginia.gov/support/facility_construction/school_construction/costs/index.shtml

We have some basic references and numbers to work with. We will need more as we go along, but let's tiptoe around the budget puddle and talk imagery.

Picture This:

From above, the Learning Center would look like a sun with 8 beams (sections) coming off it. Photo courtesy of Thevenusproject.com

There has already been some incredible design work done by futurist Jacque Fresco in his life's ambition titled: The Venus Project. Jacques work alongside Roxanne Meadows is a beautiful synthesis of form, function, and efficiency. Please check out, donate, and support "Thevenusproject.com". Learn about the ideas behind a resource-based system, and how it correlates to our predicaments today.

Upon first viewing the design looks a lot like a star with rays of light emanating from it. Jacque's design is attractive and aesthetically pleasing, but is there more to the design itself than just beauty? Radial design is a powerful tool in the public transit arsenal. No matter where you find yourself on the campus, you aren't terribly far from your destination or objective.

 Logistically, a radial design just makes the most sense. When everything is connected, permanent fulfillment channels can be established. With an automated, just-in-time fulfillment system we can minimize the need for human involvement. This will virtually eliminate shrinkage, shortages, and drastically reduce delivery times. Obviously to create a system like this, we also need a standardized warehousing and handling system. These activities should occur in an underground fulfillment center located just beneath the drop off zone. In places where underground architecture is not possible or feasible, automated warehousing facilities should be in the outer ring, but will operate slightly less efficiently.

 From a security standpoint, a radial design makes the most sense. With less distance to cover, response times will shrink. The design also does an incredible job of minimizing entry points, making access control much easier.

 From a technology standpoint, a radial design makes the most sense. Connectivity fields can be measured to the exact distance required on campus. Security tags, tracking, and personal security mechanisms can function more efficiently with this design.

 From a power generation standpoint, a radial design makes the most sense. Everything can be fed to and from a single point within the facility (with exception to the backups). With a design this integrated and large-scale, a certain amount of recycle capture can also be gained.

I could keep singing the praises of these designs, but I think I have painted a clear enough reasoning pattern on why radial is preferable.

Obviously, some changes would be made to the original design to further utilize space such as an increase in size of the central dome, entry areas for the underground transportation hub, and securing of the inner ring. These changes aside, this design is a good start for our visualization process.

Looking at the base footprint, we can simply build upward to accommodate more people. The towers and barrier rings can be built to suit. You just take the base model and add as you go! No magic, no extra planning, no fuss. Genius!

Jacque was a champion of modular design and utilizing mass-production methods to minimize build times. He knew that if we build to suit societal needs instead of our own, we could all live a much higher quality of life.

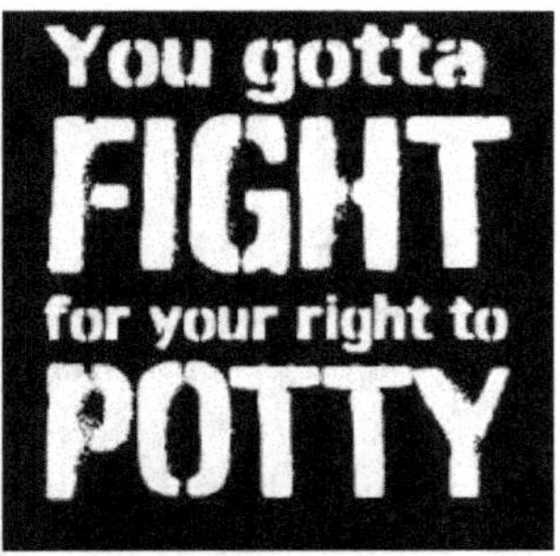

Plumbing and water collection run along the bottom outer edge of the facility to maximize access and minimize travel distance. If the crap hits the fan, it may just flow away from the building instead of into it. Having the main plumbing access along the outer edge also provides outside access to the water provider without disrupting internal activities.

 Electrical conduits should merge at the center column power storage facility and run along the inside (opposite plumbing) perimeter. This will mean that only internal staff can access the power system and battery blocks. The private power company should only have access to a digital meter on the external perimeter of the facility. Having the entire electrical system inside

the facility, along with the ability to "turn off" the grid line in case of emergency means our community has a fallback position. Remember, we are focused on securing the Learning Center power grid as its own entity. The private-bridge power connection is secondary for safety and supplementation only.

 Education is a right. With an inherent right it is vital to cut out all the middle men. I understand this will not be popular with some, but it is a necessary improvement like all the others. We have a responsibility to keep the burden as light as possible on our GDP and taxpayers.

 There is no getting around the sheer size of the facility. When people visit these monuments, they will feel like their money and efforts were well spent.

 The calculations on the next page cover the structure, inner walls, windows, HVAC, plumbing, and doors. Not included are power, water distribution, and technology systems.

Dome Stats		Beam & Tower Sections		Peremeter Ring Sections	
Diameter	240	Length	240	Length	300
Height	60	Height	44	Height	44
Stem Wall	20	Width	60	Width	80
Curvature Radius	150	Floors	3+	Floors	3+
Circumference	753.98	Floor Height	12	Floor Height	12
Floor Area	45238.93	Access Height	8	Access Height	8
Surface Area	56548.67	Sq Ft Per Section	58,910	Sq Ft Per Section	72,000
Volume	1470265	Number of sections	8	Number of sections	4
Sq ft.	90,432		471,280		288,000
Cpsqf	130		130		130
Total Cost	11,756,160		61,266,400		37,440,000
Total Structure Cost			$110,462,560		

All measurements are in feet/inches/square feet.

Land, Development, Infrastructure

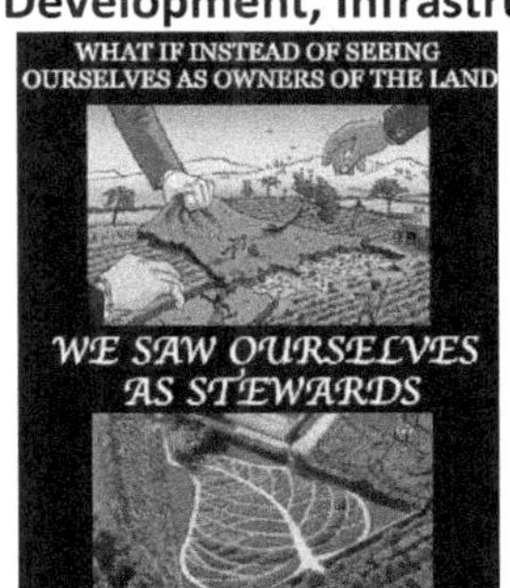

We know what it is going to take to build our shell with windows and walls, now we need the land to put it on. Because the Learning Centers will be centrally located, we will assume they will be on premium priced properties. With that in mind, we will use average commercial land costs to generate our figures.

The average cost of commercial acreage in 2018 was $18,500 per acre. Our campus should have plenty of room, about 100 acres. In areas where land is expensive, more vertically oriented versions of this layout may be considered. The cost of the land would be about $1,850,000, but of course there is additional cost in clearing and prepping the land for construction. For the additional fill, grading, and heavy lifting we will need about another $750,000. This brings our total cost for Land to about $2,600,000 per Learning Center.

We will have everyone coming to a single location which means lots of cars, buses, and pedestrian traffic. As a society we also need to begin planning for airborne traffic since the Automated Control System is set to debut in 2020.

- The ground-level, exterior-most perimeter of the Learning Center should be available for parking with a portion of the stalls equipped for vehicle charging.

- The lower (underground) perimeter of the lot should be used for unloading of passengers and freight onto automated elevators. Please note no gas vehicles should ever be allows in the sub-perimeter.

The separation of the two arrival areas increases safety and eases traffic flow. When possible, a centrally accessible mag-lev train can be run underground through the center and out into the city. Diversification of transit options will serve to further limit impact on vehicle congestion throughout the community.

Because pedestrians pose many hazards to vehicles, elevated walking paths should be provided to eliminate non-motorized travelers from vehicle transportation lots. Public transportation use should be encouraged whenever possible.

Using available figures and measurements, we can conquer the ownership of land, development of property, transportation, and the structure itself for a figure of about **$113,062,560**.

Power Systems

 Power Systems for the Learning Center are extensive and come at a significant upfront cost that is earned back in savings over time. The system will be robust, redundant, and most of all, protected from harm. Helping to satiate our thirst for power will be a plethora of solar windows, a solar-speckled primary structure, artsy wind turbine trees, 1 large and 2 smaller battery systems, 3 inverters, wiring throughout the facility, lighting, fiber optics, and technology to manage it all!

*Districts should take every step
possible to limit long-term expenses
and maximize output.*

 As a society, we need to maximize energy efficiency in every way possible. This includes running multiple lines with varying voltage, installing usage trackers that prevent non-operating equipment from pulling amperage, and conditioning only the rooms that are in use. If efficiency is planned into every aspect of the facility, usage could be as little as 40-50% of the energy use we see today.

*The Learning Center energy system
should meet the facilities entire
energy need, and possibly exceed it.*

 The LC electrical grid provides a main system and 2 backups. Any of these 3 individual systems can provide emergency power to the entire facility for several hours. In the event of a disaster, the systems can be cycled to maximize longevity of life support and filtration, thus extending protection to sheltered citizens. True security comes from knowing that you are safe, no matter what happens. (Unless the sun explodes… then we all die.)

The **United States currently spends 6 billion per year on energy for schools** and this upfront investment in renewable energy seeks to eliminate most of that cost.

For reference, total current usage breaks down to .67 cents per sq. ft. per year in electric and .19 cents per sq ft per year in natural gas.

I am estimating the usage equivalent of about 180,000 sq. ft. in solar panels per Learning Center. Any additional energy gap will be filled with solar tiles and window film. The conversion ratio for solar tile and windows is slightly lower than traditional solar panel arrays, but that shouldn't negate their use for system supplementation.

Reasoning Note(s):

- Solar panel efficiency has increased drastically due to emerging technologies.   One promising manufacturing method recently achieved a massive 44.5% conversion rating in lab testing.

- The industry current standard is roughly 25% conversion efficiency
- Conversion rates for emerging tiles and window films have recently reached the 22-25% conversion range in lab testing.
- Demand and manufacturing levels have skyrocketed, further driving innovation

Due to the above reasoning, we will use a blanket 25% conversion rating as the figure for all solar collection. If we begin manufacturing more efficient panels soon, it will only serve to sweeten the appeal.

Prepare yourself, data burst incoming:

The average solar panel takes up about 18 square feet.
That means we will need the equivalent of about
10,000 solar panels covering the Learning Center.
The average output per 350-watt panel is about 420
kWh per year when using automated solar actuators.
Multiply our 10,000 panels by the expected average of
420 kWh per. Our total expected energy output would
be 4,200,000 kWh per year.
There is a matter of loss of energy during transfer.
Adjusting 4% down for loss, let's figure an output of
4,032,000 kWh or **4.03GWh** of power production per
year.
The average price of a kWh at time of publication is
about **12 cents**.
The energy generated from our Learning Center
represents **$483,840** per year.
Solar panels are warrantied for 30 years, meaning the
expected lifetime output is around $14,515,200 in
energy.
The bulk price for installed solar panels with actuators
is about 30 dollars per square foot.
Learning Centers need 180,000 square feet which is
$6,120,000 in solar panels.

The 3 battery banks we require alongside their controllers will run us about 1.2 million each.

Let's add our battery banks for 3.6 million and our solar panels at 6.12 million.

We are all in on energy at 9.72 million.

As referenced earlier, the average school spends 86 cents per sq. ft. per year on energy total. Since our new facility will be built with efficiency in mind, we will take our previous improvement benchmark of 40% and adjust our total spending.

That brings our average cost down to 51.6 cents per square foot.

Our facility comes in at a whopping 849,712 square feet which is $438,451 in energy costs per year.

Without considering supplementation from window films and tiles, we have already achieved our goal.

You may have noticed an abundance in the energy produced when compared to what is required.

That surplus of $45,389 in energy production per year (x30 = $1,361,370)

Coupled with the overall production vs cost savings of the panels themselves over the 30-year period ($4,795,200)

Means that **EACH** Learning Center will **save $6,156,870 per 30-year period** in energy costs.

For those reaching for a calculator, it divides down to $205,229 per Learning Center per year.

We have provided the necessary power for our facility without damaging the environment or polluting the air, and we have done it by saving the taxpayers millions. In lieu of declaring victory and strutting around the room like a proud peacock, I suppose we should dive a bit more into the "particulars"

  The inherent problem with power generation systems is that they cannot provide power 100% of the time. This difficulty is magnified when you throw in the fact that societal demand for power fluctuates dramatically by time of day and year. Maintenance, fueling, scrubbing, troubleshooting, cooling, safety checks, and cycling are just a few of the standard operations in various types of plants. To ensure the population is provided uninterrupted power, we often need redundant systems that cost taxpayers millions.
 So why don't we create power as efficiently as possible, then store it in giant batteries until it is needed?
 The truth is that up until very recently our battery technology...sucked. We simply could not store enough energy into a battery to counteract its weight <u>and</u> provide the duration of use people were looking for.
 When modern lithium-ion batteries came out in the early 1990's it was a huge leap forward in duration, but the charging rates are incredibly slow, and the batteries have a slight tendency to explode when in the wrong conditions. There is also the issue of limited resources and toxic chemicals posing a limited use duration.
  Several companies seemed poised to dive into the next generation of power storage and cycling, but they are

all waiting on the technology itself to achieve realization.

Battery Banks are a big deal. They are such a big deal that even the current battery systems are worth actively using despite their downsides. We must embrace this huge efficiency improvements to our infrastructure.

Why are we dragging our feet on this?

Solid State Batteries.

A solid-state battery uses solid electrodes and electrolytes. There are no nasty liquids or polymers waiting to catch fire and explode. It also has a higher power density meaning it can store more energy. Best of all, you can open the flow and rapid-charge the battery making it friendly to high-output technologies just around the corner. Production facilities for solid-state batteries are being set up as we speak already well funded with the industries blessing.

Battery technology matters to this effort specifically because effectively managing energy flow within the facility can create significant savings when coupled with well written software. Peak demand pricing, which occurs in most areas, can be avoided entirely. Automated monitoring and flow control can be taught to "take advantage" of grid demand, and perhaps, even profit from it.

Must-do's

1. Cover the entire exposed outer surface in solar power generation mechanisms.
2. Use only multi-spectrum led lights in the facility of the same type and warmth. The only exceptions would be task specific lighting.

3. Use natural light wherever possible
4. Use natural flow where possible
5. All facility rooms should be on motion sensing and timed lighting controls
6. All technology, hardware, and machines must be run as efficiently as possible.

Water Systems

The roof angles not only serve as a pathway for the flow of heat at their peaks, they are also specifically made to guide rainwater efficiently into turbine sluices, runoffs, and grey water holding tanks. This water will be filtered by grates and stored for use to water the exterior grounds.

A note on rainwater: Collected rainwater can only be used in very specific applications but does lessen the overall clean water usage. I have heard many people complain about how the collection of rainwater is now illegal in many states.

There is a very valid reason for not collecting rainwater.

Unfortunately, we as a species release so many chemicals into the environment through dumping and contamination that the rain itself is unsafe. People often think of rain as "clean" because the oxidation kills bacteria and organisms in the air, but it doesn't break down compound synthetic chemicals. If chemicals absorb into the water and evaporate, it leads to unhealthy particulates in our precipitation, it is as simple as that.

All water for aquaponics, vertical farms, and humans will be provided by standard means, though I would urge the use of a secondary filtration system within the facility to remove the high amounts of chlorine, undesirable chemicals, and salts that accumulate in our water supply. From a health perspective, it is better for us. From an agricultural perspective it is also very important to control contaminants as they accumulate in the soil and on growing mediums.

A huge amount of funding is spent heating water for the facilities. Boiler rooms have become more efficient over the years but in most facilities the routing of the water itself isn't. If you really think about it, there aren't many places in a school that require hot water. Bathrooms (in Northern climates), food prep facilities, and perhaps a few specialty facilities. Because of the limited usage, runs can be minimized, smaller systems used, and less energy spent on fuel. Efficient, on-demand water heaters should be used to provide hot water for the facility where and when it is needed. In all cases where possible, room temp water should be used. The purest water possible should be provided for drinking. If we make sure the water is clean, crisp, and refreshing during the formulative years, healthier lifelong choices will ensue. We must be careful not to create another generation of people who refuse to drink water because they don't like how it tastes. Many in the boomer generation have come to rely on sugary canned drinks and bottled concoctions to fill their fluid intake needs. This is probably one of the biggest health issues affecting this generation.

 In the boomer's defense, many were exposed to disgusting water filled with runoff chemicals, nauseating amounts of chlorine, and goodness knows what else. We never truly shake our experiences as children, they shape our preferences for the entirety of our lives. That is why we all have family members that can't travel without a cooler.

Temperature Management

 "We've come a long way baby" doesn't even start to describe the evolution that has taken place in the HVAC industry over the past few years. Ductless systems, geo-thermal adoption, automated ventilation, learning thermostats, and usage monitoring have shown that even the biggest energy users can be tamed.

 This progression in the industry is in some ways due to its consolidation. Small mom and pop service organizations are being swallowed up by scale driven investment from the corporate sector. It is not exactly a secret that skilled trades will be the longest holdout for profitability and employment over the next half century. Corporate investment has resulted in more efficiency overall across the board. Seer ratings continue to rise which means systems are becoming more efficient. The materials used are improving alongside the automation of equipment production. Automation means fewer defects which is important with pressurized systems. The new "Smart HVAC" systems will be coming out in droves during 2018-2020. This will have a tremendous impact on the entire electrical grid because Heating & Cooling accounts for a whopping 48% of total residential use! (A few years ago it was even higher than that.)

A few notes:

- Rooms that are not in use can be shut off from the system to decrease overall demand.
- Rooms that are too far away for ducting can be zoned with ductless systems instead.
- Temperature sensitive equipment can be maintained without dramatically affecting the rest of the facility.
- Moisture control, contaminant filtering, and UV sterilization should be part of the system planning.

A note on profiteering and private interests

 Overpriced textbooks with pointless revisions forcing you to buy new when all they did was add a sentence and switch two chapters around need to go away. Who even needs a textbook nowadays anyways? Let us stop filling the landfills and start filling the desire for knowledge of our populace.

 I am not trying to make enemies of the current education consortium. Instead, I believe the time has come for a kind concession. Those who benefitted from the century of educational disarray should enjoy their good fortune and bow out gracefully.

 Those who prevent the access of many, to serve the interests of the few, are no longer welcome in human society. It is time to move on to a brighter tomorrow.

 The connections to the private sector go much deeper than textbooks. We live in a world of claimed "service rights" by corporate providers in areas such as communications, food, energy, and water. Service rights are directly counter to capitalistic principles as they eliminate competition in markets. I must very strongly assert that rights over residential and commercial interests should **NEVER** extend to the education sector. We have already shown in almost every instance that the private sector being involved in schools or prisons is a bad idea. These parasitic relationships create a situation where everyone loses, except the companies providing the service. Aside from a poor quality of service to the end-user, removing private interests from education will prevent monetary titans from quashing grassroots initiatives.

Part 14: A day in the life

To provide a better understanding of a day in the life of a student, I will outline 4 scenarios written from their 'hypothetical' perspective.

6 year old

My parents told me how lucky I am to grow up in the world today. That I will learn so much more than they could have ever dreamed of. All I know is that I love finger painting. and the big slide on the playground.

Every morning, my neighbor Lisa walks me to the bus stop. Lisa is studying to be an Administrator someday and she is always so cheerful! I look up to Lisa and know that I can ask her if I need help. She volunteers as a civilian monitor on bus trips and helps people in need. Lisa says being a monitor is great because she gets to help others, and as a bonus when she travels, she can use any public transportation for free!

When we arrive at the Learning Center, an Administrator meets us and walks with us to check-in. Kids have their own special section sealed off from the rest of the Learning Center so once I am inside, I feel safe.

I carry my badge and tablet everywhere I go. My tablet tells me how to get to my next activity and helps me stay on schedule. If I get lost or have a problem, I can always ask the hallway monitors or push my assistance button. When I get to the right room, I wave my badge in front of the door and it lets me in!

I feel like my day at the Learning Center goes so fast. On Mondays, we meet with our Team and socialize. We also learn about Team projects and competitions we can enter. My mom says your Team is kind of like what homeroom used to be but more. On Wednesdays our team works on that week's project together for an hour. I have made so many friends on my Team, and always have a ton of fun with them. The Monday Team meeting only lasts for 30 mins, then I get to go to the Art room. We draw, make crafts, and my favorite, finger paint!

After art room time, I get to go to the science lab where we get to learn all kinds of neat stuff from older students and administrators. They show us cool experiments and teach us how things work. I love science lab, it's always something new.

I start to get hungry for a snack during science lab, so after we are done, I go to the cafeteria. The team leaders always have yummy food and snacks sat out for us. We even get fresh fruit from the gardens that you see on the way in! Isn't it cool we get to eat the food we grew here?

After I eat, I go out into the kids play area for recess. The play area is fenced in and blocked off from the rest of the facility to keep us safe. There is also a cool roof that retracts so we can play outside on rainy or sunny days. They have everything a kid could ever want and sometimes, I lose track of time. If I need to get going, my badge blinks to remind me about my next activity.

After recess, I go to the math lab where I learn about numbers. I use my tablet to work through my lessons.

If I have trouble understanding or need help, I can ask the administrator or even another student!

My friend Tommy is 8 and he has math lab at the same time as me. Tommy always helps me when I need it. I am going to miss him when he moves to the big kid's section.

When math lab is over, I go upstairs to the technology room. Modules and activities in the technology lab help me learn how to use stuff. Dad says this is super important for me to learn because machines do everything for us. I just like it because we build robots and stuff. When I am in the Learning Center, my tablet charges automatically so I don't have to carry my charger.   My backpack is super cool too because it carries my belongings, water, and tablet for me.

After technology lab, I get to go to Physical Fitness. I like Physical Fitness because we do different activities all the time. We also learn how to take care of our bodies with exercise and good nutrition.

Exercise makes me hungry, so I go back to the cafeteria for lunch. The chefs make such yummy food! My mom likes it because it's healthy for me too. Mom says when she went to school food wasn't very healthy.

After lunch, I get free time. I can study in the lounge, play outside, or take a nap on the comfy couches. How I feel changes sometimes, so it's nice to take a break when I need to. A bell goes off to let me know when it is time to head to my next activity.

After lunch and recess, I go to the communications labs. Sometimes, I have trouble with my speech, so I do extra time there to help me get better. First, I learn writing and grammar with friends, then I go and visit the speech lab to work on my own. After I am all done, I go to the coding lab to learn how to make stuff with computers! It's awesome!

The last part of my day is in the Civics workshop. I learn about how my community works, and my place in it. I learn about volunteering, responsibility, and first aid. We also learn how to work together as a team to do projects.

When it is time to go home, I meet up with a group forming in the hallway. When everyone is ready, an administrator escorts us to the public transportation area. Once there, the tablet will guide me to the appropriate bus. I accidentally got on the wrong bus once and my id tag went off as I boarded. The administrator noticed and got me to the right bus. Sometimes there are no civilian monitors on the bus, but other students are friendly, and the nice security guards are watching on the cameras. They can stop the bus or make it wait if needed, it's pretty cool.

11 year old

My administrator calls me bright, my mom calls me gifted. I am graduating from the children's program a full year ahead of schedule, and I am super excited.

Until now, my days were pretty much planned for me. I got to choose a few classes, but my primary schedule was set in stone. I finished my modules early because I worked hard and have a fast-paced learning ability. I've shown responsibility, and learned the expectations placed on me. I am where I am supposed to be, when I am supposed to be there. Team members know they can count on me.

Scores from my modules, tests, and data from my personal search for who I am, and what I like to do, are being compiled for my consideration. I can use, or not use, collected information to choose my path for the future. Guidance counselors meet with me, I can ask for advice from mentors, or even other students in fields I am interested in. The decision I make isn't final, but it's nice to have direction in life.

As my parents pull up to the Learning Center, I suddenly get nervous. I've been here over a thousand times, but today is different. Today I am free to begin my own pursuit of excellence, today I begin to realize who I truly am.

I walk into the Learning Center through the entryway surrounded by plants and vertical farms. The flowers are blooming everywhere I look. Normally, I would join the group going into the children's wing, but that's not where I belong anymore. To be honest, I am not sure where I belong, just that I need to report to the Student Affairs office.

I check into Student Affairs with my badge and thumbprint. As I walk through the door an Administrator greets me and takes me into an orientation room. It is during this orientation that I finally receive my Student Technology Kit and a new badge! The administrator and I then sit down together armed with collected data from previous years. We begin discussing my strengths, possible improvements, and preferences. The Administrator walks me though creating my first education schedule and co-envision a prospective path to completion.

Everyone finishes educational phases at different speeds, and I was one of only 3 students graduating today at my local Learning Center from my age group. The Administrator had time to stay with me for 2 hours to make sure I understood everything I needed to know.

Afterwards, the administrator walked me over to the cafeteria to show me how my new badge worked. It was my first time eating in the adult café, and it was amazing! Afterwards, I joined a few others on a tour of the entire facility. It was the first time I had seen some of the advanced labs and equipment. I'm going to be using it all someday!

After the tour, I had some time before the meetup with my new Team. I decided to go sit in the common area and check out my new laptop. I excitedly signed up for my first self-paced modules and project meetings. I could've spent days just looking over all the new material, but time waits for no one.

 Having slightly lost track of time, I hurriedly pack up and head to a multi-purpose room where my new team awaits me. They are currently focused on a project undertaken in pursuit of achievement points. I sit back and watch with intent and slight awe until a tall 15ish year old boy pokes me in the shoulder. Apparently, I failed to notice his initial attempts at communication via language and flailing arms. He sees from my shiny new badge color code that I am his newest team member and takes me over to the Team Administrator. The T.A. brings me up to speed on current projects, schedules, and leads my group introduction.

 Teams help one another complete milestone projects, solve complex issues, and drive civic participation projects for the community. Outside of assigned student teams, there are also special teams that focus on specific types of activities. I plan to go to the Robot Building Team meetup on Thursday and join up because I love Robotics and Coding.

 Until I graduate from this phase, I am still not allowed to leave the Learning Center without being checked out by a guardian. If I commit to a specific activity or talk, it is my responsibility to be there. Otherwise, I spend time working on modules or in groups. When I need help, I head on over to the lab, ask a team mate or sign up for a tutor.

In the event I cannot meet my obligations, or become a nuisance to other students, I may temporarily, or permanently be assigned a case-manager to assist in moving forward.

After my Team Meeting is over, I can go home if I want, but all this excitement has my energy level high. Instead of hitting the bus, I am headed over to basketball instruction and open court time. My parents can always keep track of where I am through the app if I want to stay over.

My parents agreed to come pick me up after work so while I wait for them, and during the drive home, I work on more of my modules.

So much to do!

16 year old

Over the last 4 years, I have tasted achievement many times, and became a strong member of my community. Daunting obstacles and limitations have fallen away one by one, as I pushed to improve myself. I know what I like, what I love, and what I feel passionately about. I am prepared to take the steps necessary to realize success in my life's chosen work.

Tomorrow, I begin my path toward specialization. I know I can change my mind at any time, but it is a big decision. I am now wise enough to comprehend that I can do anything I set my mind to, but I can't do everything.

Thanks to my education, and solid guidance, I feel confident in moving onward. I have all the tools I need to achieve, and know how to get help when necessary. I know how to utilize the various components at the Learning Center to achieve my goals. I no longer need someone else to push me toward greatness, I push others.

My path toward "Leaf" specialty will be a few years long, but well worth it. When I finish, I will be ready to enter as a contributing peer in my field and begin positively affecting society. As a leaf, I shall become the productive workhorse of society, and will drive change, innovation, and improvement.

Upon arrival at the education center, student affairs pairs me with a senior student who shares similar goals. Part of my paired partners work will rely on my achievement, and I in turn will learn from this shared experience. It is an amazing symbiotic relationship that will help with my social adaptability.

*Though the system will do its best to
pair students based on personality
and interests, it may be necessary to
manually match, or re-match
students to find an optimal
partnership. Students should also be
able to request partners if their goals
are similar, and preference mutual.*

After morning meetups and work sessions, we head to the technology center where I volunteer as an assistant. Structured volunteerism allows me to gain hands on experience with the actual processes and equipment I will use later in life. In a year, I will also tutor younger students in basic technology and lab principles.

My afternoons and early evenings will now be split between group projects and personal module work. I add more and more to my already lengthy list of life accomplishments with each passing day. I stand ready to achieve as an adult, and enjoy life to its fullest. I am capable of grace in presence, and a purveyor of both educated, and critical decisions. I am the master of my life and understand the consequences of my actions.

24 year old

I just became a Flower in the field of Neuroscience. Only a select few will push themselves hard enough, and far enough to get to this point. Going forward, I will be recognized as a leader in my field. I am a verified consultant, capable of leading projects of any scale. Alongside my colleagues, I debate new ideas, review data, and devise more effective treatments. I pride myself in being an intellectual beacon, lighting the way into the future. I will do all I can to better the lives of those around me. I will mentor, cultivate, and guide the next generation to success.

Part of attainment of knowledge is the accumulation of wisdom. I hope to convey all the knowledge I have attained in the wisest and most efficient way, so that others may know. When a hypothesis is proven wrong, or in need of further research, I hope to pursue it. I pledge to remain free of bias in presentation of data for the benefit of all.

In times of hardship, I know others
will look to flowers as a leader, and I
stand ready to assist.

Part 15: Platform & App Development

Development of the platforms, databases, user interface, and global reporting network is going to take a lot of work. Thankfully, there exists a hivemind of capable souls out there in cyber space. These souls sit bored and idle, waiting for a quest such as this to undertake. And undertake it they shall. We need only create the framework and guidelines, then let the hivemind fill in the blanks. Once the system is up, passionate educators throughout the entire world can begin churning out content. Older content that is donated/gathered can also begin assimilation.

To create this masterpiece, we need a core team of passionate, agile developers. These developers should be of international origin working with minimal bias. It is important that the programs be inclusive from start to finish to avoiding risking alienation of certain groups.

Thus far we have listed a great many requirements for our new platform, and there is much left off. Even though the workload is staggering, it is no reason to bloat the workforce behind the effort. In fact, when we think about long-term security, it is important that as few people be involved in core processes as possible. Based on all the requirements we placed on the applications and software, I believe an 8-12 person project team can build the foundation for this effort. Once the path is cut, we trudge forward with the help of fellow coders around the world. Within a few years of initial public effort, we will be ready for testing.

The core team will create the secure M-V-C and necessary function maps. For security purposes, the team should encrypt and swap function names after open source code is submitted for review. This must happen with a significant check and balance system where all project members sign off.

It is important that contributors are recognized and somehow thanked for their work. Coding takes a lot of time, but much can be accomplished by someone with passion and ability. When we combine a few thousand of those people, we can move mountains. I cannot speak for everyone, but I would be hard pressed to find a majority against developing a platform enabling every child on earth live a better life.

This publication is not meant to be a rant, though I confess I feel passionately about education for all. It is in no way meant to be a commentary on the plight of the current education system or assign blame on anyone for it. The only goal of this effort is to create the next step in education, for everyone on the planet, in an apolitical manner.

As of publication, the project has already started. Once we have the funding, the project will be completed and ready for global module development and submission. While modules are being developed funding and planning for the first facility will commence.

Project Website: www.educationsolved.org

For Volunteers: www.educationsolved.org/join

For Donations: www.educationsolved.org/donate

Part 16: Startup

I confess I giggled a little when writing the word startup in a book dedicated to charitable education, but it fits. Everything consumes resources to produce output. It can't be helped. But, development of large efforts can be made much more efficient if done correctly. In this case, the development will benefit greatly early on by operating free from red tape and beauacracy. Once the basic system is created, we can use it as a springboard to national implementation. Unless this effort attracts a <u>REALLY</u> wealthy benefactor, with the resources to build the initial Learning Center, we will hope that at least one government on the planet will find this effort worthy. With a system ready to go, it would seem foolish not to.

- We know we need to build value and trust in the system.
- We must focus first on is the creation of the platform, module trees, and content within.
- If we can build the entire ready to implement system online, all governments need to do is say yes.
- Even without the Learning Centers, the online platform could provide a certification-ready home-schooling resource for the entire globe.

There is no profit or stock options in
the education plan of the future.
The development of this program
must be done for the benefit of all,
not the benefit of some.

A few dollars or a couple hours of time from people who care all around the world can get us to our goal in very little time. This is not a plea for money or a cash grab. A majority of people are barely making ends-meet these days. Please know, your time and interest are just as powerful. Talk to others, spread the word, and help change the world.

  For those involved with the development, team members would be paid the Administrator levels previously described, plus a stipend for benefits. For developers and project managers this is on the low end of the pay range, but I have seen enough interest already to be certain of participation by some incredibly talented people.

  Project stages will only move ahead once assets are available so that no effort or resources are wasted during development. Cost management & donations for this project will be public and reviewable at any time.

<u>No one will profit from this idea aside from the income they need to survive and thrive.</u>

*Outside of pay for the team, all
funds will be spent on
implementation or manifestation of
this idea.*

Part 17: The Cost, I mean savings...

*Without costing a penny more, let's
see if we can make things better
than before.*

Time to get into the numbers. As I stated previously, I will use readily available numbers from the United States for this exercise. As you will see, it can be made to fit into even the smallest budgets.

In 2010, the Department of Education spent roughly 7.3% of GDP equating to $15,171 spent per student (Student total:50.7 million) in the system per year, more than any other nation. Sadly, spending does not equate to performance. The United States fails to breach the top 10 no matter which subject you speak of.

The best way to gain acceptance of a program is to make it more attractive than the current one. Intellectual benefits aside, perhaps if we save the taxpayers enough money it will provide the momentum necessary for lasting change.

Once the infrastructure is created in the first 10 years of development, the overall cost of our new system will continue to drop. Standardization of architecture, bulk materials pricing, and machinery by lot will cause build prices to drop drastically as efficiency increases.

Personal Technology

Given current wholesale pricing on computational electronics, and the expected price drop of Standalone A.R. headsets in 2019, the cost of the student kits should be very reasonable.

Three types of kits are given during the student career. Below is current pricing in U.S. Dollars.

Basic Child Kit
Shatterproof Tablet: $350
Specialized backpack w/ built in water: $150
ID BADGE with transmitter and red alert led: $60
Water Pack & straw feed built into bottom of pack with metal protective case: $25

Student Technology Kit
AR Headset and controls: $350
Laptop w/backup battery: $450
Noise Cancelling Headphones: $75
 Backpack Case: $50

Advanced Studio Kit
Production Tower: $850
Monitor: $200
Human Interface Device Kit: $200
(mouse, keyboard, drawing pad)
The above kits should be considered gifts from society for prior achievement in the system. The gift of access and technology is an investment in our future that will pay significant dividends.
 Let's get the cost figured out per student per year to provide access technologies.

- Each student will need a basic kit totaling $585
- Each student will need a student kit totaling $925
- About half of the people need an advanced kit totaling $1250.

With maintenance and minor updates, these systems will need to be replaced every 8 years. Assuming 44 years of active use, society would replace those systems 0, 5 and 4 times respectively. This would carry a total equipment cost of $585 for the Basic Kit, $4,625 for the student kit, and $2,500 for the Advanced Kit assuming a 50% request rate. Let's heap on another $200 per 8 years in upgrade and maintenance costs, just to be conservative in our results. The grand total equipment costs per student would be $8,810 over 44 years. **That comes out to $200.23 per year per student!**

$200.23 per year to provide every child on earth (and everyone going forward,) 100% access to the equipment they need to succeed.

Infrastructure Costs Review

In our infrastructure section we went over the costs associated with the land & development of our Learning Centers and arrived at a figure of 2.6 million per facility. The cost to build the actual facility itself is $110,462,560. This brings us to a grand total cost of $113,062,560 or 113 million. The life expectancy of a properly maintained Learning Center should be about 120 years. This long lifespan is due to materials used and effective maintenance schedules. If this level of use is achieved, it would represent an effective doubling of building lifespan from current levels.

There were 13,506 school districts in the U.S. in 2002.

The current cost to build a new school system is around 103 million as shown in the infrastructure chart gathered from the U.S. Department of Education. If we take the average school system size of 2960, we can determine a building cost of roughly $34,797.29 per student served.

As stated before, the Learning Center would be serving many more students, to the tune of around 5116 <u>active</u> students. There is also the longevity factor, doubling the cost/benefit of the Learning Center. Additional service capability cast aside due to assumption, we can still lean on the life expectancy of the facility. That cuts our comparable facility cost by 50% down to 56,531,280 for purposes of side by side comparison.

If we take our cost of 56 million divided by our number of students served (2960), we come to $19,098. This represents an infrastructure **savings of almost 45% per student served or $15,699.29**. The Learning Center planned replacement lifecycle would require an allocation of **261.65 per student per year.**

Please note that this system could support as many as 25,000 or more students in a part-time or digital only role.

 I feel that it is important to once again stress the idea of universal building processes and modular components. It is important that all equipment, molds, fasteners, and local concrete mixing guidelines be standardized as well. Personally, I like the idea of using 8 giant crane style 3D extruders purpose programmed to coordinate with one another. Once you complete one building, the rest require no additional engineering, you just move the equipment to a suitable location and push start.

Utilities

  The state of Texas published an overall utility cost of $267 per student in 2014. We can use this to re-figure our utility costs. According to data from electricchoice.com overall utility usage breaks down to the following:

Lighting: 26% - $69.42 ps
Cooling: 26% - $69.42 ps
Office Equipment: 20% - $53.40 ps
<u>Water: 10% - $26.70 ps</u>
Ventilation: 5% - $13.35 ps

Refrigeration: 4% - $10.68 ps
Cooking & Water Heating: 2% - $5.34 ps

During the power generation part of the book, we showed how the power costs would not only be eliminated, but that extra energy fed back into the grid would pay for the equipment. The only expenditure we still need to pay for is water. The cost of water is $26.70 per student per year.

Transportation

We discussed several facets related to transportation of students in the previous sections. For reference, https://nces.ed.gov/fastfacts/display.asp?id=67
The reported total expenditure for the 2014-2015 school year was 24,567,019,000 or 24.567 billion. Just over half of students utilized the transportation provided at a cost of 956 dollars per student per year. This means we have roughly 25.7 million students using the system.

When looking at the cost comparison charts, we can see that a significant overall savings will be derived from system improvements. We saved 3,184,457,143 in diesel fuel because the LC will provide power for its vehicles. We saved 8,820,449,519 in labor expense by minimizing our need for bus drivers. Lastly, we shaved off 1,056,000,000 in ongoing maintenance costs. Totaled up, we saved $13,060,906,662 per year in transportation costs based off current use.

Our current cost is 24.567 billion and we saved 13 billion, in exact numbers this brings us to our new budget of 11,506,112,338 per year. This would represent an overall savings of 53.2% and equates to about $447.70 per student served.

Because we are looking at total cost per student per year, we also need the exact cost of transportation per attending student.

There were 50,700,000 reported students in our sample Current Cost is 24.567 billion equaling 484.56 per student nationally.

Versus Learning Center cost of 11,506,112,338 which breaks down to 226.94 per student per year.

Salaries & Benefits

Administrators, junior administrators, team leaders, and assistants all deserve the right to a decent and comfortable living.

The Learning Centers should operate year-round. Many school districts have already begun the movement toward year-round schedules because it is proven to be healthier for all involved. Instead of a single prolonged break in the summer, students are afforded several additional breaks throughout the year. If a student or staff member wants an additional vacation, they just schedule accordingly. Such is the power in flexibility inherent in the education system of the future.

According to nces.ed.gov in 2014 the U.S. expenditure per student for providing salaries, employee benefits, purchased services, and supplies was $11,222 per student attending public school. It represents the largest chunk of spending in the U.S. budget. The current student to teacher ratio is 16:1 or 3.6 million teachers. We will use these numbers in our final tally. Because there are a lot of extra employees and teachers in the current system, our apples to apples comparison that follows will not be used.

We used a school system with 2 elementary, 1 middle, and 1 high school in our original example. We will continue this thought pattern as we break down our current and future employment needs. The following staff are needed to run our school system.

<u>Current School System Employment</u>

- 1 teacher for each 16 students (avg $58,950)
- A Superintendent (avg $157,295)
- An Assistant Superintendent (avg $77,757)
- A Clerk (avg $37,128)
- A Principal for each school (4) (avg $88,292)
- A Vice Principal for each school (4) (avg $74,006)
- A Secretary for each school (4) (avg $37,128)
- A Guidance Counselor for middle and high (2) (avg $56,170)
- A Nurse for each school (4) (avg $49,007)
- Custodians (12) (avg $28,880)
- Groundskeepers (4) (avg $28,880)
- Engineer/Technician (2) (avg $58,641)
- Food Service Staff (22) (avg $22,110)
- Athletics (8) (avg $44,128)

Our original model school district served 2,960 students calling for 185 teachers. To serve our student body we need a total of **254 Employees** given the specifications of our sample system.

Salary amounts above do not include the standard 30% allocation for benefits which we will consider also.

Total Wages Per Year: $13,702,808
Total Benefit Estimate (30%): $4,110,842
Total Wages and Benefits Current: $17,813,650
Cost Per Student Served: $6,018.12

<u>Learning Center Employment, Wages, and Benefits</u>

Cost per student served: $5,914.64

This is the staff we need to run the entire facility. We

Salary Figures					
	Base	Adjustment %	Adjusted salary	Benefits	Benefits in $	Total Salary Package
Admin Pay	59,039	10%	64,942.90	30%	17,711.70	82,654.90
Jr Admin	59,039	5%	61,990.95	30%	17,711.70	79,702.95
Team Leaders	59,039	2.0%	60,219.78	30%	17,711.70	77,931.78
Specialists/Guardians	59,039	0%	59,039.00	30%	17,711.70	76,751.00

Departments						
	Admin	Jr Admin	Team Leads	Guardians	Specialist	
Central Planning	1	1	1	0	4	
Student Affairs	1	1	2	0	8	
Science	1	1	2	0	8	
Tech and Dev	1	1	2	0	8	
Ecosphere	1	1	2	0	8	
Math & Comms	1	1	2	0	8	
Civics & Social Science	1	1	2	0	8	
Child Services	1	1	8	0	50	
Guardians	1	1	2	12	0	
Outdoor & Rec	1	1	2	0	12	
Food & Custodial	1	1	2	0	12	
Fulfillment	1	1	2	0	8	
Artisan Skills	1	1	1	0	8	
Health & Fitness	1	1	2	0	12	Total Employment
Totals	14	14	32	12	154	262
Salary	909,200.60	867,873.30	1,927,032.96	708,468	9,092,006	
Benefits	247,963.80	247,963.80	566774.4	212450.4	2727601.8	
Total	1,157,164.40	1,115,837.10	2,493,807.36	920,918	11,819,608	
Grand Total PY						17,507,335.06

based these figures off our model consolidated school system of 2,960 students, all under the age of 18, but this center will provide education for all ages, eliminating the need for a university or community college on every corner. The Learning Center can serve up to double the number of students represented in our test sample with little to no deviation in fixed salary costs.

Discretionary Appropriations & Student Assistance

Currently there are several programs under this umbrella, the costliest of which is Pell Grants & Student Aid. The table below is available on the www2.ed.gov website. Note the table is in thousands, i.e. 30,426,028 is actually30,426,028,000

STUDENT AID OVERVIEW

Federal Student Aid Programs
(Higher Education Act of 1965, Title IV)

(dollars in thousands)

FY 2018 Authorization: Indefinite

Budget Authority:

	2017 Ann. CR	2017 Appropriation	2018	Change from Ann. CR
Grants and Work Study:				
Pell Grants				
Discretionary funding	$22,432,626	$22,475,352	$22,432,626	0
Mandatory funding	7,897,676 [1]	7,950,676 [1]	7,055,000 [1]	-842,676
Subtotal, Pell Grants	30,330,302	30,426,028	29,487,626	-842,676
Federal Supplemental Educational Opportunity Grants	731,736	733,130	0	-731,736
Federal Work Study	987,847	989,728	500,000	-487,847
Iraq and Afghanistan Service Grants	442	442	499	57
TEACH Grants [2]	153,342 [3]	153,342 [3]	24,572 [3]	-128,770
Total, Grants and Work-Study	1,873,367	1,876,642	525,071	-1,209,884

NOTE: Table reflects discretionary and mandatory funding.

[1] Amounts appropriated for Pell Grants for 2017 and 2018 include mandatory funding provided in the Higher Education Act, as amended, to fund both the base maximum award and add-on award.
[2] TEACH Grants is operated as a credit program. Amounts reflect the new loan subsidy, or the net present value of estimated future costs.
[3] The FY 2017 amount includes a net upward reestimate of $138.4 million due primarily to assumptions pertaining to the number of grants that will convert to loans. The amount for FY 2018 reflects new loan subsidy.

As you can see 32,302,670,000 was spent on Federal Student Aid Programs in 2017. There is also the matter of the student direct loan program which racked up 26,833,498,000 in spending to provide students with the additional funding necessary to cover skyrocketing university costs.

The truth is that the Learning Center provides post-secondary education with the costs already figured into our previous considerations. Learning Centers will eliminate student debt, loans, Pell grants, and Military Education Funding because there will be no need. Anyone who wishes to further their education will do so freely. We will go more in depth on the topic of default savings in Part 18.

We will kick 20% of our Discretionary over to a Special Projects Fund for communities, eliminate the Loans program, and save the taxpayers billions.

Innovation & Research

The funding for Research and Development funding by the U.S. government in 2018 is around 176.8 billion dollars. I do not wish to haggle over this number, nor consider it in our final tally. Instead, I hope to see this funding used as efficiently and effectively as possible.

Special Education Programs

Special Education Programs are a tricky subject when it comes to both current and Learning Center centric educations systems. I do not pretend to have all the answers on this subject and a final consensus would need to be found. The above acknowledgment noted, I would like to put forth the following observations and recent data driven realizations:

- Current Special Education Programs are required to cast a wide net in attempting to educated children with various, and sometimes conflicting disorders.
- Determinations need to be made on a case by case basis for viability of student ability.
- A Universal System cannot have deviations. We would need to immediately eliminate honorary,

- special, and "bestowed" types of awards/degrees.
- Because of the sharp rise in Autism and other Learning Disabilities, it is possible that young children could be grouped in hopes of promoting growth and positive behaviors.
- At around age 8, a determination will need to be made on a case by case basis to make the right path forward for the student.
- Because of the self-motivated nature of the Learning Center program, consensus would need to be found on how best to care for individual's incapable of normal participation. This consideration seems outside the scope of our focused education initiative.

Special education finding in 2014 was 30.5 billion. There is a potential for savings, but I cannot speculate as to exactly how much because the numbers available are cryptic and difficult to get hold of specifics on. The best way to tackle this issue is with great guidance counselors and open communication with the student & guardian.

Food

In 2014, the U.S. spent 12.7 billion feeding roughly 30 million children per day. Each Learning Center will produce a small portion of its own food but outside support is obviously still necessary. No child should go hungry in a country as advanced as ours. If a child is enrolled in Learning Center activities, they should be fed and well cared for. This is what people in society want. Even the most hardened fiscal conservative would agree that children should not suffer starvation due to their situation. I am going to leave this figure alone with the hope that we will use the funding more effectively instead of squandering it on distributors and middle-men.

Ongoing Maintenance

A study on Gssaweb.org states the following costs per student for ongoing maintenance factors as follows:

- Trash Collection/Waste Disposal 12.44
- All Maintenance Equipment & Supplies 67.03

By minimizing waste and controlling logistic packaging, some of the waste costs can be curtailed, perhaps by about 15%. For maintenance equipment and supplies, our costs will go down. We have a large facility, but many of the contents are designed to last a long time. Although dependence on chemicals will be reduced, dependence on filtration of both air and water will be increased. I will leave these adjustments up in the air until data guides our path forward.

Technical Education

The demand for skilled technicians continues to rise as robotics removes the monotony from our lives. The safest jobs over the next 50 years will be engineers, digital creators, programmers, skilled tradesmen, and contractors. Children with even the slightest gifts toward these skillsets should be guided toward them. It will soon be our greatest need, and hopefully we can avoid an upcoming skills crisis.

Billions are spent both privately and publicly on these skills. Training availability is lacking. We are wasting a ton of effort and funds for little return. The Learning Center can provide centralized training and qualification services throughout all these industries. Exact figures were nearly impossible to find online, so I can't add the tremendous savings we would attain as a country, but it would be in the range of 25-45 billion per year in the U.S. alone.

Facility Technology

We are technology. Mankind can no longer function without it. Our future will revolve around the technology that makes us comfortable, healthy, and happy. The best way to breed innovation and adept users is through active experience. When a new technology is introduced to an industry, it needs to immediately be introduced to the Learning Centers as well. Obviously, there would be a vetting process for this, but it is imperative. It is in the best interest of technology manufacturers to provide these technologies in bulk for minimal profit or even, at cost. The reason for this is that familiarity with students leads to market saturation down the line. People will always use what they are most comfortable with.

We currently spend about 56 billion dollars per year on education technology breaking down to about $400 per student per year.

As shown earlier, our student kits would cost about 200 per student per year. The rest of the budget should be allocated to usable technology within the Learning Center. This is one of the few areas that could even see a slight increase in funding due to impact. For now, we will leave it as it is, utilizing all we can in hopes of growth.

Continuing/Post-Secondary Education

I save adult education for last because it is a primary crown jewel of my argument for education reform. Nothing in my life has disturbed me more than the face, and ineptitude of adult education in the United States.

In fact, I would argue that it is the leading monetary predator of our lives.

The United States spent 559 billion dollars in 2015-16 school year on postsecondary education. Yes, half a trillion dollars. The United States spends almost $1500 per citizen per year to provide mediocre education returns.

The Learning Center would eliminate 85% (475.15 billion) of this expenditure because students all the way up through Leaf (Masters) level could easily achieve without leaving their local L.C.

The remaining 15% (83.850 billion) could be used to create specialist facilities where flowers and candidates could further societal research in a focused and efficient environment. These focus groups could be used to create international cooperation in a field and familiarize leaders with one another in hopes of fostering ongoing communication throughout their lives.

Part 18: Conclusion

Our stated goal was to create an outline upon which a new education system could be forged. It was important that this change be attractive in both effectiveness and cost. It is obvious that the Learning Center system would provide more opportunity, better education, and more effective resource utilization, we need only address the issue of numbers. As stated previously, the spending on education is horribly murky with large estimates often being the only data available. Instead of providing a final budget number, I have decided to provide a final savings number. As you will see on the next page, no matter how argumentative you want to be, there is no getting around the numbers. I left out all factors we called even or re-allocated.

Out of our Federal Education Budget, we can save 341,682,652,782 or 55.6% of current expenditures. All told our system will save taxpayers 1.351 trillion per year in total expenditures.

- Taxpayers save money
- A MUCH better education is provided
- Opportunity will no longer be limited to the wealthy
- Staff members are paid well with great benefits
- Education never ends
- The population is prepared for the next step in societal evolution
- We can rebuild our communities one seminar at a time

Total Spending and Budget of all factors (not including Post-Secondary)			769,169,700,000
Current Budget cpy			15171
Student count			50,700,000
Total Number of School Districts			13,506
Sample Size			2,960

Description	Current Cost $	Current Cost Per Student	LC Cost $	LC Cost Per Student PY	Difference $	Difference CPY
Infrastructure Costs per district	103000000	579.95	56,531,280	261.65	46,468,720	318.3
Utilities	13,536,900,000	267	1,353,690,000	26.7	12,183,210,000	240.3
Transportation	24,567,000,000	484.56	11,506,112,338	226.94	13,060,887,662	257.62
Salaries and Benefits	568,955,400,000	11,222	299,872,248,000	5914.64	269,083,152,000	5307.36
Discretionary Appropriations & Student Assistance	59,136,168,000	1166.39	11,827,233,600	233.28	47,308,934,400	933.11
			Total Savings off Current Budget		341,682,652,782	7,056.69

Additional Savings by Proxy

Description	Current Cost $	Current Cost Per Student	LC Cost $	LC Cost Per Student PY	Difference $	Difference CPY
Technical Education	30000000000 est	591.71	included	0	30000000000	591.71
Continuing & Post-Secondary Education	559,000,000,000	11,025	83,850,000,000	1,654	475,150,000,000	9,371.79
			Total Savings off Current Budget		505,150,000,000	9963.5

Grand Total All Savings	1,351,982,652,782	26,983.69

If you are still with me, thank you. Like any human, I am flawed, and I know that somewhere in this book you probably disagreed with me. The important thing is that we have began a conversation promoting improvement, and the conversation now has a basic framework. But this is not the end. The effort to make this education system is ongoing, and it needs your help. Please visit www.educationsolved.org and see how you can help us make the world a better place. I welcome your constructive criticism, ideas for improvement, volunteerism, and donations toward this universal cause.

<u>Please help us.</u>
<u>If you have an idea, share it</u>
<u>If you have an edit, write it</u>
<u>If you have a contribution, bring it on.</u>

We can change the world by
changing the minds of the people

www.ingramcontent.com/pod-product-compliance
Lightning Source LLC
Chambersburg PA
CBHW061801250726
48657CB00001B/236